GENDER EXPLORERS

Gender Explorers

Our Stories of Growing Up Trans
and Changing the World

Juno Roche

Foreword by Susie Green
Afterword by Cara English and Jay Stewart

Jessica Kingsley Publishers
London and Philadelphia

> **Trigger warning:** This book mentions suicide.

First published in 2020
by Jessica Kingsley Publishers
73 Collier Street
London N1 9BE, UK
and
400 Market Street, Suite 400
Philadelphia, PA 19106, USA

www.jkp.com

Copyright © Juno Roche 2020
Foreword copyright © Susie Green 2020
Afterword copyright © Cara English and Jay Stewart 2020

Library of Congress Cataloging in Publication Data
A CIP catalog record for this book is available from the Library of Congress

British Library Cataloguing in Publication Data
A CIP catalogue record for this book is available from the British Library

ISBN 978 1 78775 259 7
eISBN 978 1 78775 260 3

Printed and bound in Great Britain

Dear trans folk,
We are changing this world for the better,
never let anyone tell you otherwise.
Walk tall, aspire and dream.
With love and respect,
– Juno

Foreword

Nearly twenty-two years ago, my life changed, pivoted completely, based on the trust placed in me by my then four-year-old child. This was a time when trans was not a part of my vocabulary. I had no clue whatsoever, comfortable in my ignorance, considering myself to be open-minded and fair. Nothing prepared me for what was to come, how that moment would change everything.

To place some context to the social environment at the time, films like *Crocodile Dundee* and *Ace Ventura*, which openly mocked trans women, were considered the height of hilarity. I knew, peripherally, about transgender people, referred to as transsexuals at that time. What little I knew was coloured by those films, the media portrayal of men in dresses with beards. That transgender children existed was impossible to me, not that I ever actually gave it a thought. Why would I?

My daughter is now twenty-six. When I talk about her words to me that morning, that simple sentence: 'God has made a mistake and I should have been a girl,' I still experience that visceral reaction, despite having recounted that moment so many times over the years, explaining why I am so passionate about the work I do, previously as a volunteer for many years and then, more recently, as CEO of Mermaids. The fear for her. The rush of adrenaline, that made it difficult to speak. The denial in that moment of what she was telling me, and for her, the betrayal of her trust in me. It took another two years before I listened properly, something I deeply regret.

When Juno asked if she could talk to me about the possibility of a book based on the actual words of trans kids and their families, I knew there was nobody else that I would trust with such an important task. Her writing is eloquent, brutally honest and manages to bridge a gap between ignorance and understanding, which I think is so important.

We discussed how this might be achieved, and the weekends that Mermaids holds for families around the country were an obvious fit. Those spaces are so valuable. Safe. Joyful. Sometimes painful, because the absence of judgement and fear can sometimes bring to the surface things that by necessity, have been buried. We discussed the format, context and how it might look. Juno came to a few weekends, and spoke to many children, young people and their parents.

When she sent me the manuscript to review, I suddenly found myself back in the room, twenty-two years ago, reading other parents' reactions. Some were very different, but for some, it was me, again, sat on the sofa with my beautiful little girl. Hearing her truth for the first time.

The one thing that shines through all these personal stories is love. Because of this, I am hopeful of a better life for the children and young people we support. I see the discussions around transgender children being woefully ill-informed.

Sensational, misleading, judgemental and unkind. And then, I read this, and I know that this is what we need to see, not people talking about trans kids, but people talking to them, and their families.

Things are very different to what they were twenty-two years ago, where the only information I could find was a paragraph in a book about 'girly boys', that stated they were probably gay. Young people can see themselves in popular media such as Hollyoaks and Emmerdale. The internet has removed some of the isolation and stigma, but we have a long way to go. This book is another step towards understanding. We have hope for a better world for these amazing children and young people who continue to astound with their courage and clarity. We need to listen and respect them. Only they have the right to say who they are.

Susie Green, CEO, Mermaids

About the Book

This book isn't about proving or disproving, believing or disbelieving, challenging or not challenging the validity of trans children and their parents or carers. These young people are me, and for a brief summer term in 1972 I was them. They know their truths, I know our truths, and no one can tell them, or me, otherwise.

This book is concerned only with listening to young trans and nonbinary people tell their own stories, without judgement or adult intervention; hearing them offer advice. As adults we've had years of gender conditioning that makes us want to order the world in a way that we understand, but this is not necessarily a way that works for us or for others.

This book is a recipient of these young people's joy and also a conduit for hearing and learning about the difficulties they might face – arising principally, I'm sure, from the discrimination and disbelief meted out to them by disbelieving adults who are shaped by the narrow confines of gender expectations, stereotypes and binaries.

We can and must learn from these young people if we

want to create a kinder world which enables all children to dream and aspire; which enables all children to shape gender comfortably so that they can treat others, the planet and their own futures with the dignity and respect that is far too often lacking now in a grown-up world shaped by the pain of gendered stereotypes and expectations.

This book has a simple remit: to allow them, the young trans and nonbinary people so often talked about, the space to talk to us.

Use it or we'll lose it and we'll lose them in the process.

Introduction

Just to be completely crystal clear and not leave a single shred or sliver of doubt in anyone's mind as to why I'm writing this book, I will start by saying this: *I believe that children who are questioning and exploring their gender, or simply making gender do what they need it to do in order that they can lead happy, functional and aspirational lives, are the future of this planet. They are the gender explorers and gender bosses that we all so desperately need.*

Yes, I feel as strongly as that: *I believe they are our future.*

Deep down in my sassy trans soul I believe that trans, nonbinary, gender fluid and gender nonconforming children are wonderful beings who will reshape and perhaps even save this planet from the mess that so many older people (and sadly some younger) have foisted upon it. I have every faith in them, whereas I have far less faith in people of my own generation and older.

Deep down I believe in trans children. Not only do I believe in them, but, more importantly, when they talk to me, I listen to them, I hear them and I believe them. If they tell me they are a girl or a boy or neither or sometimes a bit of both, I don't question them, *I just trust their truth.* I listen. In writing this book I had the pleasure and privilege to *listen* to and *hear* many of them.

Deep down in my fizzing, blooming-brilliant trans core I believe that this small group of often slighted, maligned and misjudged children are both unknowingly brave and generous and are demonstrating to us how we can, might and should control the alignment of our gender from the outset.

In teaching parlance, *they are leading by example* and modelling how to approach gender with tenacity, grace and control. They are doing this in a world which frequently creates a climate of fear and panic for them to grow up in. Thank the goddesses for the *parents, carers, caregivers, support groups, teachers and others* who surround these young people with love, creating a barrier to all the toxicity.

I talk a lot – many people say I talk far too much – but when I am in the presence of young trans children and teenagers I'm often silenced by the way that they are navigating the complexities of life itself and handling the complex pressures of gender expectations and stereotypes.

The pressures are most often coming top down.

In the course of writing this book I had the chance to travel the country and interview many trans and nonbinary children and teenagers and I was constantly amazed and often stunned by the kindness they demonstrate and exhibit towards a world which so frequently treats them very badly. They simply see themselves as trying to be the best that they can be and trying to be true to their innermost feelings. They often readily forgive the world for treating them so badly.

Again, in teacher speak, *they are trying to live up to their potential.*

I'm someone who transitioned late through a formal, medicalised and often punishing process demarcated by stages of negative and positive interventions. This process only began after spending many unhappy years hiding the truth of my gender misalignment because I wanted and needed to please the world around me that was constructed upon a binary patriarchal thinking. It's taken me years to live up to my true potential.

I sometimes wonder if the word 'transgender' applied to a five-year-old who is determined to be themselves, whatever the cost, makes any sense in the way it does perhaps applied to me? They are merely expressing their gender, or expressing their sometimes tentative, sometimes bold, enquiries and exploration into gender. After speaking with many young trans children and teens I wonder if the word 'transgender' applied to them isn't a tad misleading as they are just being as they need to be. For them there is often no transitional process as I perceived and lived it, but often a joyful, playful journey from the get-go towards their authentic core. They leave a starting point with a determination to be themselves from as close to day one as possible.

If supported and simply allowed to be themselves, their journey feels natural and ordinary. 'It's just normal,' many of them said to me.

It's often the 'grown up' intervention that creates the environment for depression, darkness, sometimes suicidal ideation and perhaps even *attempts*. When the loaded label *'transgender'* is applied to a five-year-old who is just being true to themselves I'm not sure that the label works to create any positive framework. One parent told me that her daughter didn't really know or understand the word 'transgender' until she was ten, when it felt important, politically, that she understand the context for the discrimination that might come her way. The word 'transgender' as a conduit for discrimination.

I like the terms *'gender boss'* or *'gender explorer'*. That isn't to say that these young people don't have to engage with a process (sometimes medical, often therapeutic), but if the starting point is joyous and determined, then the process is entirely different from the one we more closely associate with the label *'trans/transgender'*, which is applied to those of us who transitioned later in life.

From the outside these young people may appear to be products of patriarchal and socialised patterns of gender expression: 'I felt like a boy', 'I wanted to climb trees', or the classic 'I like pink'. But look a little closer and you will see the marvel of a human, a tiny human, grappling with and bossing gender from the outset, saying, 'No, you'll do what I need you to do. Forget all those people around me telling me I'm wrong, telling me I should be this way or that. I want to be happy, not sad, and I want to express myself the way that feels right for me.'

Sometimes they come out quite brilliantly and succinctly by sending an email which announces their gender intent. Sometimes it's via a carefully planned letter. Sometimes it's conveyed through tears and sometimes with anger. But the one thing that is clear to me from my gender travels with this brilliant group of children and young people is that at the same time that they are thinking about what they need to do to be their authentic selves they are also thinking and caring deeply about *how to protect those around them that they love* – their families, carers and friends.

In their letters they often include a list of *go-to places* for information (there is also a list of Resources at the end of this book). Can you believe the kindness and generosity inherent in that act? Can you imagine being eight, ten or thirteen years old and writing the most important words in your young life, yet thinking as much about the people around you as about your own inner turmoil?

These children's souls have silenced me.

They should be silencing any naysayers.

Look closely at them and their lives and you'll see such an incredible capacity for kindness, strength and bravery, as well as a rock-solid commitment to be the best that they can be. In that simple, often slight act of picking up or putting down a toy, you will see an epic change happening in society, one that has the capacity to benefit everyone. One that allows everyone the opportunity, the space and the freedom to make this thing that we call gender work for us all. The change is a ripple that can't be held back. *It's pure change-energy* that is already covering much ground. Ripples with the power of tsunamis.

We live in a patriarchal world in which stereotypes – pink, blue, dolls, tanks and toys – are still so rigidly fixed that they dominate not only our high days and holidays but also the humdrum of our everyday existence: school uniforms, career expectations, colours, clothes and body adornment. These gender explorers can only select the items that line their walls, their shelves, their toy boxes and the world they move around in – shops, schools and their homes. They cannot create a new world of *gender parity* in *gender materiality* until we let them. Trust me, in fifty or a hundred years' time, gender expectations, stereotypes and fixed gender positions will be utterly unrecognisable if only we support these children to be themselves. They will loosen the insidious grip of gender harm that holds tight around all of us. Often fluid and unfixed, their young understanding of gender creates spaces that never existed before. *They are a new phenomenon.*

If we support these gender explorers, they will reshape our environment to allow for far greater freedom and fluidity. They, along with others, will eventually do away with the meanings that we grew up with, meanings that absolutely and punishingly boxed us into different lines and categories. Our architecture is already changing: school buildings, changing rooms, more spaces are rightly becoming gender neutral. Clothing is no longer something that needs to be divided neatly along gendered lines, and that doesn't mean shapeless grey hoodies are gender neutral!

Young gender bosses and explorers are silently changing the very landscapes we move through, be that buildings, ideas, language or economic values. Nothing can remain the same if we support them and *allow them to flourish.*

Until we live in a world which isn't divided by gender, we cannot blame these children for adopting 'our' gender signifiers to express their gendered truths. We mustn't get caught up in debates about how these children are really just butch girls or feminine boys and how they are destroying the queer landscape. Quite the opposite, they are stretching the queer and non-queer landscapes to include many more people. We may laugh at the endless Facebook profile options, but we hated being boxed into the two rigid categories of male and female. Those two categories extinguished so many of our gendered identities.

Some trans adults, but especially these younger gender bosses, are widening the suffocating narrowness of what it means to be human in the twenty-first century.

When I first to tried to truly express my gender *at eight years old*, I was told I was *not fit for purpose*, that I was *not capable of knowing my own mind*. Back then there were no words to describe people like me – not in everyday use anyway.

I thought I was the only one like me on the planet who felt one way inside but looked another on the outside. It must be a terrifying feeling to find yourself living with this in the contemporary contentious and adversarial battleground around gender and trans lives.

To feel that your innermost self is entirely different from the way the world sees you is *terrifying*.

Back when I was a young person, the world kept us feeling like we were few and far between by treating us very badly, almost extinguishing us by turning us into a rare mental health classification. If we were apparently rare, then we could live in fear that we were the only one like us.

Being trans was considered an illness. We were seen as ill, as broken, as needing a sex change. If we got into the right line and stayed on our best behaviour, then someone would eventually come along to help repair our broken bodies. It was seen as an act of charity: of helping a sick individual to be *patched up*; of helping them to make the most of a broken life.

Those days are gone. Sorry (not sorry), but they are gone. The ripples we have created, the ripples that younger gender bosses and explorers are creating, demand that we be treated with *respect and decency*. The ripples are changing the environment for younger and younger people to express their gender authentically within; it's becoming a little easier for them. *Thankfully.* So, the numbers of younger people coming out are rising; it makes sense, *doesn't it?*

It is a safer space now, one defined in great part by greater understanding and respect.

It seems simple.

These young trans and nonbinary people are managing to ignore the enforced dominant script of gender over which we have no control and are writing their own scripts from scratch to fit their lives. They are resolute in wanting to *be the best that they can be and they want to be happy*.

And they want to be happy *now*!

Just happy.

They want their present, *their now*, to be positive and happy rather than having to close their eyes and dream about a future in which they might get to run away and become themselves. As I did. Dreaming for years about being the me that no one could see.

These children and young people are the true superheroes of our age (not the ones populating the Marvel universe).

I feel sad that I can't truly identify with them because my journey to my trans authenticity was full of *trouble, strife, struggle and fight*. They are defined by being in the moment as themselves whereas I lost almost *half of my life*.

Through the process of speaking with many young trans

folk in the course of writing this book, I have had to own the subtle feelings of sadness I have, but also the feelings of slight envy. I'll never know what it is like to live most of my life authentically, I lost so much time, so many potential experiences and memories that I will never know. *Years of missing photographs.*

But, overriding this sense of sadness and envy is a sense of joy that these young people can be the best that they can be at an age before the real mental harm and anguish can grow and embed. These young people owning and bossing gender, despite the attacks and mistrust, are what being alive should be about. *They are building joyful lives. They are life. They understand life. They will be the ones saving the planet.*

I'm not claiming for a second that they have idyllic, perfect lives. We only have to look at the ill-formed prejudice in the media to know that cannot be true. But when these children have loving and supportive families and encouraging and committed teachers and safe and inclusive schools then, *yes,* for many of these children there is little struggle, only joy. I know I've heard them talk their truths and I've seen their smiles. *Great big real smiles.*

I cannot comprehend my identity without the absence of struggle as my identity was shaped by struggle and pain. My body is literally shaped from a hormonal and medicalised battle for my *space* and *wellbeing.* But I do know how it feels to *'just be myself'* because at the age of eight I had a few glorious weeks in which I was able to be me, *just me.*

And I was ridiculously happy. In those few weeks I was overcome with the joy of being alive. If I close my eyes now, almost fifty years later, I can still remember that feeling.

That joy. I smiled and laughed, and I ran into my school eager to put my hand up in class to answer questions. I was confident, I was engaged in my life. Before that time, I'd never put my hand up in class because I couldn't stomach the world noticing me. In those few short weeks I decided that I wanted to be a writer. It took me over thirty-five years to get to write again, to see that it could happen.

I was born in 1964, and the first time I ever emerged as myself was in the school playground, aged eight, in 1972. I had the briefest moment of being me and then the world told me that being me was a huge problem and one I should deal with by not being me and by *pretending to be someone else*.

My dad liked cowboy films, so I tried to be a *cowboy*.

The Most Wondrous, Spectacular and Smiley Pansy!

Pansy came into being in a sunny school playground in 1972 – the summer term, to be precise. I don't remember the exact day or time, but I know it was during a playtime which narrows down the time of her birth should we need to do an astrology birth chart. Pansy emerged, laughing and defiant, into a crowded playground full of laughter and noise. The playground was surrounded by grass, and on one side sat the school building. By the end of the summer term the grass had turned straw-yellow and was replaced by brown swirling dust. It was a warm summer.

Our school was a late-1950s building, with all the classrooms leading off from a small central hall in which we sang cheerful songs, learned the Lord's Prayer and jumped over low beams, pretending to be either deer or dancers. It was the age of *Top of the Pops* and Pan's People. We all wanted to be a dancer in Pan's People; at least I did, and boy did I learn the moves (not that there were many moves, just lots of *finger on the cheek pouting*).

Pansy emerged whilst we were playing Kiss Chase in the playground, possibly after finishing a small bottle of warm milk from the wooden trolley that the milk monitors pulled around to each class just before morning break, rain or shine. Rain was better because the milk was at least slightly cool; in the summer it had often curdled, and you'd only find out after whooshing it down through a paper straw. Before the afternoon break, we'd have a cup of warm orange squash and a biscuit, often a Custard Cream or a Jammy Dodger.

The moment that Pansy first emerged I was running away from the boys in my class (although I'm not sure that they were chasing me). They were chasing the other girls and trying to plant weird bird-like peck-kisses on their cheeks. We were very young, so Kiss Chase often ended up in Trip-Up or Tag. The boys laughed at me running away from them (in their eyes pointlessly) and called out to me, 'You're not a girl, you're not a boy, you're just a pansy, a stupid little pansy.'

Over, and over again, they hurled what they imagined was a great insult at me, designed to make me come to my silly *pansy senses*.

Instead, I stood rigid-still as it dawned on me that I was Pansy. Not a pansy, but Pansy. In that one insult everything in my unhappy and confusing life became clear.

(Thank god for the boys!)

I turned to the boys, who were now beginning to form a bullying, fight circle around me, and said, 'I am Pansy, and I like it when you call me by my real name.'

I spun around 360 degrees and kept on repeating, 'I like it when you call me Pansy.' Like a seven-inch disco track, I spun until I felt sick. I was so happy that I'd made myself want to throw up joyful vomit.

The boys roared with laughter at me spinning around but then as they dispersed and ran away, they shouted back, 'She's Pansy, Pansy, Pansy, not a boy, not a girl, but a stupid Pansy.' They said other stuff, not-so-nice stuff, but I only heard 'she' and 'Pansy', and I thought, 'I'm taking it, it fits.' It was the first name, label or insult to ever make me feel warm inside, a little like now when someone calls me 'trans' or 'queer' and I think, 'Perfecto – too right I am.'

Importantly, it was also the first time I'd ever been called 'she', a pronoun which back then lifted me up, rather than 'he', which pulled me down.

As a young kid I never understood why 'he' didn't work, or why my old name (which was Simon, in case anyone cares) didn't work. When people said 'he' or 'Simon', I could see the words leave their mouths, travel towards me, hover in the air in front of my eyes and then fall to the floor. I spent my childhood trying to pick my name up off the floor and stick it on my forehead. The name I was given at birth was the one that never worked for me.

Simon, Simon, Simon. Repeat after me, 'You're *Simon, Simon, Simon.* And *Simon* is a "*he*".'

After that brief, idyllic summer of Pansy I'd have to wait years to be seen and properly addressed again. I'd have to wait years to allow Pansy to grow and become happy. Stuffed down under layers of shame and self-hatred and the name Simon, which was the only name I was allowed to exist beneath. But it was never my name. When people said 'Simon', I never felt seen or understood, *I felt invisible.* Worse, I felt that I didn't exist as a human alongside other humans because my birth unintendedly stripped me of my humanity.

But for that single summer term in 1972 most of my classmates, enemies and friends, called me Pansy. Many used the pronoun 'she', but not all, and those that did often hurled it as an insult which I caught between my teeth as small uncut diamonds. I swallowed the diamonds and they amassed deep inside of me. For years those diamonds and the memory of that summer term kept me alive through so much trouble and strife.

In that summer term I felt free and I felt confident and I felt alive.

Plucking up courage, I asked my teacher, Miss Honey, if she would call me Pansy like everyone else did. She hesitated, turned away from me and looked out of the window towards the old weeping willow tree. She then said that *during story time on the carpet I could be Pansy if I liked and if I behaved well.* I always did. As an eight-year-old I thought that maybe all the answers to difficult questions might be found from looking at that weeping willow tree.

On the round, quite threadbare carpet in our classroom I listened to stories and poems and grew to love words, associating them with my freedom, happiness and safety. Miss Honey never said 'she' but used 'Pansy' enough when addressing me or talking about me to the class to allow me to believe that this happy feeling might become my life. I adored the way that Miss Honey read stories and made them come to life. The stories she read became more and more real and as they did, so did I.

Away from the classroom carpet, Pansy loved doodling and drawing and wished that she could fly up to the top of a tree and make a nest, like chimpanzees do *(but she hated heights and couldn't even climb to the top of the climbing frame, let alone climb the rope when it came out during gym).*

Pansy loved being outside and loved nature. Pansy had a pet toad that she secretly carried into school; a pet toad that she wrote stories about; a pet toad that she drew pictures of in different outfits – flares one day and a pinafore dress the next. Pansy dreamt about becoming an explorer or an artist or a poet.

Pansy also wanted to be a mother.

When Miss Honey asked Pansy what she wanted to be when she grew up, in front of the whole class she replied that *she wanted to have a belly full of babies like her mum.* My mum only had the one baby in her belly at a time, but to Pansy, to me, pregnancy was a magical thing and to Pansy anything seemed possible: a belly full of babies or a toad who could talk and travel on a plane to far-off countries; a toad with a passport. If Pansy had become *real* and *happy*, then *anything* was possible.

Towards the end of that summer term Pansy had *one hurdle* to overcome. She had to convince her family to call her 'Pansy' and 'she' if they wouldn't mind. 'Simon' and 'he' made her feel very unhappy and confused. Although her family might be upset about the loss of her name, *she thought* they would be happy that she was finally happy and no longer *a quiet and shy loner*, as people had often referred to her when they thought she couldn't hear.

Pansy waited until the end of the summer term, thinking it would be better to raise the issue at the start of the holidays. Perhaps she'd ask them in their new car, a red Capri, on a day trip to the sea (to Sandbanks in Bournemouth, which was the most exotic place she'd ever seen – her dad had said that it was like Hollywood).

Everyone in the family adored that car – flame-red and as fast as a rocket.

Driving, we'd listen to a cassette tape of The Stylistics or Diana Ross, and Pansy would crouch down on the floor in the back, push her head forward between the two front seats and sing for everyone. She knew all the words to every song. She felt safe with her family even though she often heard them whispering about her, using the word 'effeminate' and saying it wasn't right that a boy would do *this or that* or not do *this or that*. She didn't care. She was Pansy now and one day she'd make it onto a stage and sing for everyone, like Karen Carpenter or Joni Mitchell (although I never played the piano or the guitar, just the recorder badly – 'Three Blind Mice').

Her family loved her singing and she loved performing.

There is a photograph of me as a young child with long blonde hair, way down past my shoulders. Tied around my waist and shoulders, like an outfit from Mary Quant or Biba, were West Ham football scarves that my dad was desperate for me to bond with. I did in my own Pansy way. Looking back, I don't understand why the world didn't understand what they were looking at. It was blindingly obvious. I look at that photograph and only I understand how happy I could have been and how many years were lost to unhappiness.

I decided to tell my dad and older sister about my new name on the driveway next to the car. We were getting ready for our day out to Sandbanks. I was stood one side of the packed cool box and they were stood the other. It was a completely unintentional placement.

It took all of about three seconds for Pansy to be slapped away – just one quick, hard slap. It only needed one to make me feel stupid and clumsy again. A good telling-off followed and a lesson about boys being boys and girls being girls and pansies being pansies and not Pansy.

'Never let anyone call you a pansy, do you hear?'

It was the early 1970s. My family didn't understand; they were just worried that I'd get beaten up, picked on, or worse, bullied every day for the rest of my school days, which happened horribly to a few children who for one reason or another stood out. I was bullied anyway, whatever my name. My family couldn't see how happy I was to be Pansy. For them, gender was set in stone at birth and was rigid. If anyone, especially their child, strayed from that (presumed safe) rigidity, then all hell would break loose.

They told me that if anyone called me a pansy again, I should come home and tell them so that they could sort it out. All of my family could fight apart from me. The last thing I wanted was for anyone to be beaten up for calling me a name that I liked and wanted to use myself. In my dreams I called myself 'Pansy'. Should I tell them so that they could beat me up?

By the time I returned to school in the autumn, Pansy had all but disappeared, retreating deep inside of me. I disappeared with her into a pit of unhappiness that would last for many years and at times become so devastating that it resulted in self-harm and addiction.

By the time I returned to school, I'd returned to silence. I never put my hand up in class again and when Miss Honey read a story on the round, threadbare carpet, I put my hand into her bag and stole a packet of sweets. Hard-boiled toffee sweets. I stole them one by one until she saw me. I wanted to be seen.

She told me off, called me 'Simon' and sent me to see the headmaster, who said that *he'd never seen me outside his office before and that it was out of character for me to be in trouble. I should think long and hard about what I'd done and never do it again.* 'Where was the smiling child who'd left at the end of the summer term?' he asked with resignation.

Confused and filled with sadness and anger, I decided there and then that if I couldn't be happy, I'd steal sweets and then steal more sweets until there were no more sweets to steal. And I did. From that day on, the day I was called 'Simon' again on the carpet, I behaved terribly at school.

I never thought back to that summer term in 1972 again. A term when the sun was forever shining. A term when I was so excited to go into school that I ran so fast one day that I tripped over and hit my head on the main school door. I had to have ten stitches, that's how excited I was to be me and to be free.

That's how excited I'd been to be Pansy.

How Did I Go About Writing This Book?

For a year I attended a series of weekend family residentials with the charity Mermaids and I also attended a series of Saturday youth clubs with Gendered Intelligence.

Mermaids is a charity set up to support trans, nonbinary and gender nonconforming children, young people and their families to achieve a happier life, often in the face of great adversity. They campaign for the recognition of gender dysphoria in young people and call for improvements in professional services.

Gendered Intelligence's mission is to increase understandings of gender diversity and to support young trans people through a wide range of youth work provisions and activities.

The two sets of interviews were very different in structure and time. The Mermaids interviews were spread across a weekend and feature not only the young people but also some parents and carers. The Gendered Intelligence interviews fitted into their quite amazing youth club parameters and feature only the young people (no parents or carers).

With complete kindness, generosity and a faith in my ability to write their truth(s), both groups allowed me into their fabulous worlds to sit and listen and ask questions. I spoke with young trans children (the youngest being five), older trans teens and some young people in their early twenties. It felt important to have some follow-on into higher education and perhaps aspirations beyond. I listened as they told me about their happy times and the times that weren't so happy. I listened and then cried afterwards, alone. The Mermaids team must have thought that I was a little anti-social because after each day of interviews I would eat a little, walk a little and then go to bed.

The process made me both happy and sad. It was cathartic. It made me think about my own childhood and how cruelly, perhaps unwittingly, I'd been treated by a world not ready to listen.

I apologise to the Mermaids team if I seemed a little quiet, but in those interviews I captured a world in which trans and nonbinary young people and their parents are, by hook or by crook, making their lives work and allowing slivers of happiness to grow. I've never seen such nurturing from anyone. One parent described her role as being like that of a meerkat, on constant alert, watching out for aggression or danger, and at the same time finding the time and strength to create a safe space for their children to play and to grow up in.

In the Mermaids interviews I really wanted to focus on what was happening at school and in the education of the children. In my own very small way, I felt a little like a teacher-meerkat and I wanted to see and highlight the good and also the damage done to children's education when we listen or don't listen to them, when we support or don't support them. Education is just a way to dream about the future and explore the present. To dream is to aspire. To dream or aspire you have to be present in the 'now'.

I hope in the process of writing, I've captured some of this.

For the Mermaids interviews I used the same room each day. I stayed put and used the same question format to start the interviews. I always worked backwards towards the word 'trans' with the younger interviewees. Sometimes we rested at superpowers and that was more than enough. Sometimes they told their truth with a maturity and sensitivity that would silence much of Twitter. With the older ones we sometimes started with the word 'trans' and worked outwards to where they needed the interview to go.

There was nothing prescriptive about the interviews. They started within the same space and with a similar format but went towards their own truths.

If the parents or carers were up for chatting, then I interviewed them afterwards. They were always present when the under-sixteens were being interviewed and could stay if the over-sixteens felt comfortable. It was often the first time the parents or carers had heard the young person's innermost thoughts. The interviews were joyful but also full of tears.

Make no mistake: these meerkat parents and carers are superheroes. Rather than mistrust them, we should only seek to offer them support.

I am in awe of them all.

The Gendered Intelligence interviews were structured differently to the Mermaids interviews. For my first visit to their Saturday youth club I simply observed their methodology and working structure(s). I had time to understand and appreciate how they work as an organisation and how I might come along to a session and, without impacting on the space, collect some interviews. For the book to be rounded it felt imperative to collect interviews from both organisations, Mermaids and Gendered Intelligence.

Therefore, getting it right and fitting into the Gendered Intelligence model and being able to utilise the far shorter time frame was paramount in getting the right kind of interviews – interviews that reflected their ethos as well as the grander themes.

Since I had far less time to conduct the Gendered Intelligence interviews, these interviews are much shorter than the Mermaid ones. I enjoyed the challenge of working differently. The week I attended to carry out the interviews, there was a theme of 'self-care'. It made sense to loosely pitch the interviews around this theme and to focus on why this group mattered to them as young trans and nonbinary folk.

I thought long and hard about whether the interviews should run as a single block rather than separating them out by organisation, but the structures were so vastly different that it felt only right to reflect that in the actual physicality of the book. One set had time and space – I had a room and the time to speak with parents and carers. The other set of interviews was principally about collecting the voices of the young people, with very little intrusion on my part as a writer. Both methods had their own merits and outcomes. I suspect they add to the pace of the book in the same way that the different organisations add huge value to the landscape for young trans and nonbinary people in the country.

I came away with the lasting feeling that however we as adults organise the world, the young people themselves are very similar, whichever structure they find safety and joy within. The joy is quite literally bursting from the spaces created by both organisations. The work they do is epic!

Interviews: Part 1

These interviews were carried out with young trans and nonbinary people and their parents and carers during the Mermaids weekend residentials.

Trans Girl with Identical Twin Brother

How old are you?

Trans girl: I'm seven. We're [*looking at her brother*] twins.

Are you identical twins?

Both: Yes.

Let's talk about superpowers. If your sister had a superpower, what would it be?

Brother: I think it would be telekinesis and heat breath and freeze breath.

What does telekinesis mean?

Brother: It means you can move things around.

If you were going to move something around with the power that your brother says you have, what would you move around?

Trans girl: The furniture.

Would you change the furniture in this room?

Trans girl: Yes, I would put that chair over here [*she indicates to the chair her grandma is sitting in behind her*]. I would put it so that I could see her. But I think she is happy where she is.

Do you want to move it?

Trans girl: No, I think she is happy where she is.

If you could give your brother a superpower, what would it be?

Trans girl: Superspeed.

What good things would you do with your superpower or superspeed?

Trans girl: I'd make people dizzy.

Is that a good thing? I'm not sure I'd like being dizzy.

Brother: I would speed up buildings and I could catch my sister as she's the faster runner. She's got lots of medals at home for running races.

How many medals have you got?

Trans girl: I've got three already. By the time I'm twenty, I'll have sixteen medals for running.

I think that my superpower is being trans. Why do you think that I might think that?

Trans girl: Because you are trans and it means that you can be whoever you want to be.

Is it a good thing to be able to be whoever you want or need to be?

Trans girl: Yes. Being trans is my second superpower.

How do you think your trans superpower has helped your classmates?

Trans girl: Because now they can be who they want to be and not be someone they don't want to be. Instead of feeling sad because they can't be who they want to be, they can now be who they want to be and be happy.

What's most important do you think: being happy or being as fast as a cheetah?

Trans girl: Being happy.

Where are you happiest in the world? I'm happiest in my house in Spain because I get to see my dogs. When they first see me, they wag their tails so hard that I think they might fly off! That's when I'm at my happiest. Where and when are you happiest?

Trans girl: At school with my brother.

Is he the best brother ever?

Trans girl: Yes.

When are you happiest [to brother]?

Brother: When my sister is around me.

If you had to pick a few words to describe your sister, what words would you pick?

Brother: Intelligent, clever, very brave. She faced her fears.

When you started on your journey, what were your biggest fears [to the trans girl]?

Trans girl: That people were going to laugh at me.

Did anyone laugh at you?

Trans girl: No.

That's because you're brilliant and frankly a superhero. How did having your brother with you help with that fear about people laughing?

Trans girl: If people ever bullied me, he'd stand up for me.

Brother: It was quite scary for me when my sister first went into school as herself. I had to be brave. I was scared that people might bully her or just laugh. It happened a little bit at first, but I stood up for her.

Are you proud of your sister?

Brother: Yes, very. But I'll get prouder of her if she gets more medals for running.

So, when she's got sixteen medals, you'll be really proud?

Brother: No, only when she's got ninety-nine medals.

How would you describe yourself now [to the trans girl]?

Trans girl: I'm happy, caring and I think I'm quite popular.

Have you got any idea what you want to be when you grow up?

Trans girl: A fashion designer.

What kind of clothes do you want to design?

Trans girl: Wedding dresses.

When I was a teacher, there was a small group of children in my class who told me that I'd be happy if I got married, so they designed me wedding dresses and the dresses got bigger and bigger and bigger. It was a little like Juno and the Giant Peach.
What do you want to be when you grow up [to the brother]?

Brother: I want to be a pharmacist.

Who has really helped you on your journey [to the trans girl]?

Trans girl: My brother has helped me the most.

So, having a brother who stands by you and helps you has been important?

Trans girl: Yes.

If you were going to give any advice to somebody else starting out on a journey like yours, what might it be?

Trans girl: Be brave and don't let anyone bully you. And try to be whoever you want to be. Ignore the bully and walk away and tell the teacher.

Thank you, both of you, you are brilliant.

Twins' Mother

Can we think back to that first day when your daughter went into school as her authentic self... What were your feelings as a parent?

Mum: It was more me worrying about her. It wasn't about my feelings. I was worried about the reception that she and her brother would receive – if there would be any bullying or ostracising, that kind of thing. But I felt quite secure in that I'd done quite a bit of groundwork first, so I'd been into school, explained the situation. The teachers were fantastic and were onboard and wanted to do anything to support me my way, which I was adamant about – it needed to be my way.

What did your way look like? If someone was reading this and thinking, 'This is exactly what's happening in my life and I need to make sure this is done properly, my way', what might your way mean in relation to other people?

Mum: So, my way is about personalising it for your child. You know your child more than anybody else, so it must be about them. They, the school, might have a perception of how they are going to deal with it, how they might handle it, which might not fall in with what might suit the personality of the child. Because my child was so young at the time – five – I knew that the children might not get the concept, so I took some children-friendly books into school which could be read with the class as stories, which they were. The school were good in that by the first day that she went in as herself in her proper girl's school uniform, her name labels had been changed on her peg and schoolbooks, and the register had also been changed. The children had been told in simple, age-appropriate terms that some children don't feel like what's in their head matches their body, and it was explained to them that for my child this was the case. The simplicity of the explanation meant that her peers just accepted it and moved on.

More important was picking her and her brother up from school that day. Both myself and my husband picked them up and took them to school that first day. We needed her to know – and her brother – that we were there for them both; it was such an important day, a milestone. The teacher took us to one side and said that it was like having a completely different child in the room. She used to isolate herself all day in the dressing-up corner. But now she was answering questions and being confident enough to run around outside, she was playing with everybody. Some of the boys who used to pick on her because she'd be in the dressing-up corner in a dress stopped bothering her.

People sometimes make this whole process so complicated. If you could give some simple advice to other people, what might it be?

Mum: Embrace it. Embrace it even if you're frightened of it. It's the only way to control that fear.

* *

Trans Girl

First, can you tell me how old you are and what pronouns I should use?

Trans girl: I'm eleven and 'she' and 'her'.

Are you in the last year of primary school?

Trans girl: Yes, I'm in Year 6.

What's your favourite thing about being at school?

Trans girl: I have no idea; I just like being there.

Do you have a favourite lesson?

Trans girl: Art is my favourite lesson. My favourite thing to sketch is people.

Are you good at drawing people?

Trans girl: Not exactly.

Have you ever drawn a self-portrait?

Trans girl: I've tried.

Did you put it on the wall?

Trans girl: No, it didn't look good, I drew my nose over here [*points to her cheek*]. It looked a bit like a Picasso.

Can you remember back to the first time you went into school as yourself?

Trans girl: Well, it was last year, and a royal wedding was happening. I went into school in a black-and-white dress. It had flowers on it. The school knew I was going to. I felt happy.

Did you have any fears at all?

Trans girl: I felt happy, but I had some fears. I was happy because I was going in as me. At home I had always been me, dressed as me.

When you walked into school on the day of the royal wedding, how did you feel inside – being able to be yourself?

Trans girl: It just felt normal. It felt like it was the way it always should have been.

After that first day, did you stay as the real you in school?

Trans girl: No, because I didn't have the right uniform, so I kept going in like before. I got a dress and then on the following Monday I went in as me. It just felt completely normal to me.

So, if you were going to give anyone in your situation any advice, what would you say?

Trans girl: Be yourself and don't let what other people say bother you that much, otherwise it will put you back.

Does it ever hurt if people say anything nasty to you? If people say anything horrible to me about being trans I ignore them because being who I am makes me feel strong and beautiful.

Trans girl: When people are being horrible to me it's because they don't understand. I ignore them but I wish I could change the world. I get to be myself and be happy now.

When you grow up and start working, do you know what you might want to do?

Trans girl: Sort of. I want to save animals.

Do you think that being trans will hold you back in any way?

Trans girl: No, I think it pushes me forward.

If you could say anything to the world about being trans, what might it be?

Trans girl: That they are happier being themselves and that it's selfish making us wait until we are older to be ourselves.

Why is it selfish?

Trans girl: Because they are saying that we can't make decisions until we are older, but I'm happy now.

I don't think I've spoken to anyone who puts it as beautifully and simply as you. Thank you for a lovely interview.

Trans girl: You're welcome.

Trans Girl's Parents

Listening to your daughter talk about going into school that first day, she talks about it feeling normal. What was it like for both of you?

Mum: It was quite emotional, but the school have been fantastic with us. We went to pick her up, but the only thing she was worried about were her shoes hurting her. She got the dates and days slightly wrong. She went in as herself a couple of weeks after the royal wedding day.

Dad: It was after that half term.

Mum: Yes. There were a couple of weeks when she dressed as herself at home and playing outside. We thought she'd go in as herself in the following September, but in the half term she said she was ready. We were like, 'Fair dos, she's ready.' Over the half term we went out shopping to replace her uniform and then realised that we had much more to change that would remind her and her classmates of her previous time – her pencil case and other stuff. Much more than you think to make sure she would be comfortable.

But the difference in her was massive. She'd been such an angry little child. She suffered from such rages, didn't she?

Dad: She did.

Now?

Mum: We get occasional strops but nothing like before.

Dad: The rage is still there, but there are big spaces in-between – like months.

What made it easiest: her being so matter-of-fact or the school being supportive?

Mum: We were lucky that the school were really supportive, but we were lucky that we had some information from Mermaids that we could go into school with. We felt forewarned and went in with our backs up, ready, but we didn't need to. Thankfully. When she told us we thought, 'Okay.' The school said they weren't surprised – it made sense. The difference in her happiness is huge. The in-your-face anger has disappeared.

How has that impacted on your family? What does it mean to have a happy trans kid?

Dad: It's like a weight off our shoulders to have that anger explained. The anger was directed at everybody.

Mum: And over nothing. It would literally appear out of nowhere. It's just gone. She said she just feels normal now. She's happy for people to talk. There was a girl at school who made some comments. The school dealt with it, but she said, 'It's not her fault, she doesn't understand.'

Dad: She's so laid back with it, she'll talk with anyone.

How do you as parents get support? Do you need support?

Dad: We haven't really. I'm not sure we needed it. I don't think we've needed it. It's been a breeze really.

Mum: She's so much happier. We had an angry little confused boy and we now have a happy, vibrant and confident daughter. We couldn't ask for anything more. She's happy, our home is happy, it's perfect.

* *

Trans Teen Who Identifies as a Non-Stereotypical Girl

Where would you say you are happiest?

Trans teen: Either Crewe train station or the viewing place next to Manchester airport or at Disneyland Paris.

Why are those your happy places?

Trans teen: I have a big interest in trains. Me and my dad used to go there all the time. We sometimes still go. At Crewe it's a junction and there are six lines that meet there. It's interesting. I can identify trains by the sound of them. I can do that with airplanes as well.

So, with your eyes closed, if a train passed here now could you tell what kind of train it is?

Trans teen: Yes, of course.

Disneyland Paris feels different.

Trans teen: I'm obsessed with Disney. I especially like the animated classic films and the Pixar films.

What's your favourite Pixar film?

Trans teen: *Ratatouille.*

I once saw all the original Pixar models for the films at an exhibition. They were beautiful. Does animation link into a future career that you might want?

Trans teen: No, I want to be a stock trader.

A stock trader – like stocks and shares? Why stock trading?

Trans teen: I have a big interest in maths and that's a maths-heavy career. It's like a dull stable career.

Did you enjoy being at school?

Trans teen: It was alright. I always had friends I knew I could go to and depend on.

Did you express your gender at school?

Trans teen: I came out in Year 9 and came back in Year 10 as me.

What was that like?

Trans teen: When I first went back in the door I was terrified, but soon I realised that everyone was nice about it. Even the people I was expecting to not have nice reactions didn't seem to care.

So, what you expected to happen and what did happen were

completely different. If someone were reading this and they were expecting the worse, what would you say to them from your experience?

Trans teen: Society is progressing at an astonishing rate. I'd say don't be afraid to come out and try to be as open as you can be. Try not to get defensive. It's hard but try not to. If someone asks you a question and you don't feel comfortable to answer, just tell them you don't feel comfortable with their questions. Sometimes people are scared about asking questions. I'd say be approachable as it might make your experience better, easier. Maybe it's even helping our wider community by educating them and stopping them from getting bad information from bad sources.

Do you feel that you are making a difference to the world?

Trans teen: I guess. I try to be open – not if someone asks me something too personal, but I want to break down stereotypes, so I speak up. I think breaking down barriers is important. Being trans doesn't define me. I'm not going to just become super-girly. If someone buys me anything sparkly for my birthday, I just think that's really wide of the mark. I still wear men's jeans. I'm a girl but not a girly girl. I don't let being trans define me. I am my own person. I make my own rules.

Who helped you the most to get to this point?

Trans teen: I can't attribute it to one person. I could probably narrow it down to close family – for example, my mum [*turns to mum briefly*]. She was very supportive when I came out. She said, 'I don't have the information but I'm going to educate myself so I can be there for you.' It led her to work for Mermaids.

But my grandad has been one of my favourite people since I was little. He was part of the reason I connected to trains and planes. People say that the older generation won't understand or be accepting, but he couldn't be more accepting. He and my nan are so chilled about it. Mum told them because I was too scared to be in the room and I was sat on the stairs outside the room. Grandad was like, 'There's nothing wrong with that.' I almost started crying because I knew it was going to be so much easier than I'd imagined.

But the other person who's been helpful has been my closest friend who I've grown up with. She'd always be there for me. If I had trouble explaining something, which I sometimes do, she'd say, 'Don't worry, take your time.'

I had a friend at school who transitioned and made it seem so straightforward. Before then I'd really struggled. That friend really helped.

You are a great interview; I know you were worried about talking. If you could time travel back to the you in Year 7, what would you say?

Trans teen: Society is moving really fast. You're transitioning and being trans doesn't have to create any barriers for you. Don't try to force yourself into any gender stereotype. When I first came out, I tried to please everyone by being super-girly but then I gave up. I saw my old men's jeans and I thought,

'They're convenient, they fit and they have pockets.' I've been wearing them ever since. Just be yourself; and if anyone asks you why you aren't being stereotypical, just say that being trans is about overcoming stereotypes. Just live your best life.

I'm blown away by your words, thank you.

Trans Teen's Mother

Can you remember your daughter coming out to you?

Mum: Yes, it was the day that David Bowie died.

How did you feel?

Mum: To be honest I'd always been waiting for something. A lot of people around us assumed she was going to come out to us as being gay. As her mum I knew it wasn't that. I wasn't sure what it was. I was in my bedroom reading. No, actually before then I'd suspected that she might be trans, so I organised a trip out to see the film *The Danish Girl*. I pretended to have a spare ticket so she could come along.

But the day that she came out I was sitting on my bed reading and she came in, sat down and said, 'You know that film, *The Danish Girl*, well that's me.'

So, I said, 'You feel female on the inside?' And she said, 'Yes.' I asked her what she wanted to do about it, and she said she didn't know. I said, 'We can find out.'

Your reaction was very matter of fact. Why do you think you took it in your stride?

Mum: When I was seven... [Pause.] Do you remember *The New Avengers?*

Yes, absolutely.

Mum: At seven I said that I wanted to marry Purdey. I had the Purdey haircut. I used to practise my Purdey kicks. I didn't know then that I was bisexual. I didn't know the words and I'm never sure what my word is. But my older sibling, who was nine at the time, took me to one side (being an older protective brother) and told me that I couldn't ever say that. He told me it wasn't allowed and that I'd get my head kicked in. It was the early 70s and he was probably right. It was an incredibly homophobic time. But at seven years old to be told that something that just feels like the most natural and beautiful thing is not only wrong but could put you in danger... What do you do with all those natural feelings at seven? Well, you push them down and down until you get a knot. I think every LGBT adult knows deep down when they got their knot.

I call it my Purdey moment.

Because I was waiting for something with my own child, I was constantly remembering my Purdey moment and I was just determined that, whatever it was, she was not going to have those feelings. When it came to her making her social transition, it was a case of 'You are either 100 per cent positively onboard or you are out of our lives. I don't care who you are, you are out of our lives.' It mattered so much to me that whoever she is, it is right. Not even up for discussion.

That's such a powerful message, that Purdey moment and not wanting someone else, your daughter, to have that moment. I had my own Pansy moment at eight years old. If somebody hasn't had their own Purdey moment, what would you say to them? How would you explain or express that moment to them?

Mum: I don't know. You can only go on your own childhood experiences. When a child comes out to a parent, we are all experiencing that from completely different starting points.

So how might you explain how that knot feels?

Mum: It feels like sudden, instant anxiety that something awful is going to happen any second, but it's a permanent state. Most people only experience that for a few seconds. But when that's a permanent state in your life, it feels over-whelming. But I also thought I was the only one because back then in the 70s there were no lesbian or bisexual women anywhere – they didn't exist. They weren't in books, in films or in *Coronation Street*. I thought I was the only one who felt like that, so I felt like there must be something wrong with me.

If there were a scale of one to ten for that pain (ten being the most painful), where is that pain on that scale? What does that pain physically feel like?

Mum: A ten. Physically it feels like butterflies in the stomach, but not in a nice way.

To me it felt like a crow flapping wildly inside me. That horrible feeling of unrest. If you could give any words of advice to a parent who may be going through this process, what might they be?

Mum: I would say that you never get a second chance at a first reaction. Put love first, unconditional love first. Anything else can be worked out.

* *

Trans Boy and His Mother

Thank you for taking the time to chat to me when you could be outside playing. Can I firstly ask how old you are and what pronouns you use?

Trans boy: I'm fifteen and I use 'he' and 'him' pronouns.

When did you first tell anyone in this big confusing world of ours that you might be... Well, actually, how did you first say it? Did you say that you thought you were trans or that you were a boy?

Trans boy: I don't know, I think I might have told my sister first when I was eight, but just before that I was at a family event and hanging out with other boys and I told them that I was a boy and they said, 'No you're not.'

Can you remember back to how it felt to tell people?

Trans boy: I'm not sure it felt like anything.

Can you remember how it might have felt when they said, 'No you're not a boy'?

Trans boy: It felt funny because it was a funny situation. We were very young.

When did you first come out at school?

Trans boy: In Year 8, at the beginning of Year 8. People kept asking me if I was transgender. People on the other school bus that I wasn't even on were talking about whether I was transgender. People were having conversations about me and asking me on the internet and asking me in real life if I was a boy or a girl. I thought, 'This is too much. I should just tell people.' Then I started going to school as me and told my friends and my teachers. The school changed the register and it was smooth really.

It was that straightforward and simple?

Trans boy: Yeah.

Amazing. If there was someone else in your position at the start of Year 8, like you, what would you say to them? I imagine they might be scared and anxious.

Trans boy: I would say that you can't get hung up on how you are going to do it. It must work for you. You must be safe but also take things in your stride. Get support and deal with any bullying by talking to your teachers. But you must be strong and go through with it, for you. You mustn't accept or put up with any bullying.

How did you make sure you were safe?

Trans boy: I wasn't really threatened at any point but I did get questions that I didn't like and I had to move on from that. Sometimes I ignored it. One of my teachers spoke to a couple of my friends and asked them to keep an eye out for anything. I thought that was a really nice gesture.

Did you go home and talk at home with Mum?

Trans boy: I don't remember, do you [*turns to Mum*]?

Mum: Yes, I'm not sure I handled it the best. I know you're not really interviewing me yet.

No, that's fine, please carry on.

Mum: Okay. I think he tried to tell me by saying that he wanted to be 'he' at school and I said, 'I don't think you can do that.' I was quite resistant.

Trans boy: Yes, I think there were quite a few times when I asked you to call me 'he' and you said you couldn't. You said, 'We're not ready for that yet. You need to find a proper therapist.' You thought it was too big a step.

Mum: I did. My memory is that you sent me an email saying that I had to listen to you. I'm sure I've still got that email somewhere.

Trans boy: You can delete it if you want.

Mum: The gist of the email was, 'Mum, you're not listening to me. This is my story.' I sat up then and started to take notice.

How did you become or remain so calm and quite brilliantly together enough to be able to send an email saying, 'You must start listening to me, Mum'?

Trans boy: It just seemed to make sense. I don't think I was being strong. It just seemed like the next logical step.

You were being strong, brave and epic. The fact that you underplay it is a testament to your brilliance. The fact of putting words down and sending an email might be useful for someone who might read this and be struggling to talk.

Mum: It shut me up and made me listen until he stopped speaking. It was brilliant. The school contacted me and said did I know that he had been into school and told everybody he's 'he' now. My child has been into school and become themselves and I didn't know. I was so impressed by his strength. He just started to use the boys' changing room. He took matters into his own hands. He knew that if he asked the school they might ponder and panic, so he just said what he needed and got on with it. He thought he was going to make it simple and just do it.

Trans boy: When I first went into the boys' changing room I said, 'Does anyone have a problem with me being in here?' Everyone said, 'No, no problem.' Then I just got changed. When I told you, you said that they might have a problem but not say so, but I said I knew they didn't.

Had you ever heard about trans people or trans issues?

Trans boy: Yes, I knew. Initially from that CBBC thing, *I Am Leo*, and then from reading about it on the internet.

⚘ *What was the most useful source of information for you?*

Trans boy: Stumbling across a trans boy my own age. I was eleven at the time. I'd only ever heard of trans adults or older teenagers. I found a trans boy my age who I started talking with, and through them I found a trans camp that I went to. It was finding that acceptance and permission to be trans while at a younger age that really helped me to transition.

How does being trans feel to you?

Trans boy: It just feels normal really. I'm just a person. People sometimes say that you shouldn't transition unless you absolutely need to, but to me it was an incredibly positive thing. Why should you have to be able to deal with the maximum amount of dysphoria before you act or do anything? No, transitioning is a positive step that allows you to be accepted as you really are. Transitioning shouldn't be a last resort but a positive step towards being happy in your life.

People of my age sometimes had lifetimes of unhappiness and dysphoria. People said to try anything else but transitioning. It makes me very happy to know that you and others won't go through that.

Trans boy: It has been hard sometimes but being able to be myself is so important. I sometimes thought that it was a shame to be spending money on transitioning when it could be spent on other fun things, but without transitioning I couldn't properly enjoy anything in my life – not if I was living my life in the wrong gender.

Do you have any idea what you might want to do with your life?

Trans boy: Something to do with science. It changes every week, but sometimes I like Chemistry and sometimes Physics.

It would be wonderful if the career you choose could take you in a direction where you are able to change the world for the better so that more people can experience what you have experienced and how you have done it... You are incredibly smart, intelligent and so grounded. Interviewing you has grounded me. If you could take your brilliance and change the world to make it easier for people, what would you do?

Trans boy: I'd like to become a doctor and help trans people. I'd also like to work on climate change. Things could be a lot better.

Who are the people who need to get stuff better?

Trans boy: Everyone.

How do they need to get it better? If you could write down one thing and it could come true, what might it be?

Trans boy: That's a hard question.

It doesn't need to be a right answer. Just say what comes into your mind.

Trans boy: I would want everyone to understand that being a person is very broad. Things you experience as a person – be that putting on a sprinkler in the back garden on a hot day and running through it to cool down, or skiing – are all individual experiences that we go through. I would want everyone to realise that trans people go through those too and need to get on with living just like everyone else. We just need to live our lives.

Yes, I moved to the mountains just to walk in them with my dogs. Just to do the stuff in my life that I want to do.

Trans boy: I recently told someone that I was transgender. He was very confused by that and said, 'Does that mean that I need to see you as a girl as you were once a girl?' I said, 'No. Some people are tall, short, transgender or ginger. Being trans is just like that, just one thing about me. I'm still the same person you know today. I was a girl and now I'm me and happier as I am.'

Was there a moment when being a girl stopped working for you?

Trans boy: Yes, when I was in Year 7 and we were doing an online quiz in class and it asked for my gender. I said, 'I don't want to put female because it doesn't feel right.' My friend said, 'Just put "male".' I did and it worked, it felt right for me. It was the beginning of Year 7.

I love how you responded to what was happening. Such a role model. You seem to trust that you know what's best for you.

Trans boy: I'm trying to live my life really.

Are you happy?

Trans boy: Yes.

Where are you happiest and why?

Trans boy: I'm happiest when I'm having fun. There's a proverb – I think it's Chinese. It says that to be content in life you need someone to love, something to work on and something to look forward to. If you've got those things, you'll be happy. I was happy this morning when we went swimming in the river with people from this residential – that was fun.

Just being in the moment and swimming.

Trans boy: It was cold.

I bet.

* *

Trans Boy

Can you tell me how old you are?

Trans boy: I'm eight years old.

Do you like school?

Trans boy: Yes.

What's your favourite thing to do at school?

Trans boy: I like Maths because I'm really, really good at doing Maths. I like all of Maths.

What do you think you could do with your brilliant Maths ability?

Trans boy: Maybe build buildings?

How fabulous. Does being good at Maths feel a little like a superpower?

Trans boy: Not really.

If you did have a superpower, what do you think it could be?

Trans boy: Dancing. I like watching people do the Cha-Cha.

Can you do the Cha-Cha?

Trans boy: No, not really, but I can do the Floss. I can do it really fast.

Where are you happiest in the world?

Trans boy: With my friends, playing games we like to play.

What kind of games do you play?

Trans boy: Any game – outside usually.

Do you have lots of friends at school?

Trans boy: Yes lots.

You sound very popular. Ever since you've been you at school, have you always been happy?

Trans boy: Yes.

What are the best things about being you?

Trans boy: Having a brilliant mum and having a 'boyday' for when I became a proper boy.

As well as your birthday?

Trans boy: Yes.

Who has helped you the most to be this happy as yourself and at school?

Trans boy: My mum and dad, they listened to me.

If you could say something to other parents of children like you or me, what might you say to them? Just a small piece of advice?

Trans boy: Treat your child as best as you can.

Trans Boy's Parents

Can you remember back to when your son told you or the moment at which it came to light?

Mum: It was gradual.

Dad: *There were lots of clues.*

Can you describe some of those clues?

Mum: At first, it all seemed to happen with me. The verbal stuff happened with me and I remember the first sentence. He spoke a lot of words, he was quite a late talker, but the first sentence that he strung together was literally, 'Why wasn't I born as a boy, Mum?' I thought that was a bit peculiar and I filed it away in the back of my head and tried to forget about it. But then it kept coming, the same story, the same question, time and time again.

As a trans person I can't imagine what it's like to hear that question from your child. What is it like to hear that question?

Mum: It's confusing, very confusing. I started researching.

Dad: I didn't.

Mum: He [*looks at husband*] buried his head in the sand.

Dad: I didn't create any friction but I ignored it.

What was the emotion?

Dad: He would always dress up at every opportunity. At birthday parties, at his own parties, on days out going to the soft play area, he'd dress up in different superhero outfits. As a superhero he could pretend to be a boy without anyone challenging him.

Mum: It was more than that, it was every day when he got home from school – straightaway he would change into his costume: Spiderman first, then Captain America, then Batman.

Dad: There was Ironman for a time. Basically, anything to get out of his clothes. Once he transitioned, he never dressed up again.

Mum: Batman never appeared again.

Dad: He never touched any of his costumes again.

Mum: We went to a local LGBT group, a brand new one for

kids, run by a woman who has a trans child. When we went along to that, they asked, 'What do you want to be called? He said "Batman".' This was before he socially transitioned. He was still she. But then after socially transitioning, Batman never appeared in the group again. I didn't even realise at the time, the group leader had to point it out to me.

What was the emotional response from you once he transitioned?

Dad: I just felt relief because I used to take him (back then, her) to school every morning. Every morning he'd run through the gate, run up to the door and then stop short of the door. Every morning he'd stop, and I'd have to talk him into school. Every morning it was like that until he transitioned and then he just ran straight in without stopping. I think I was a little bit scared and a little bit hesitant and worried about confronting the whole subject, but as soon as I opened my eyes to the subject it became completely clear.

Mum: This went on from the age of three, that's when it started. At the age of five, nearly six, before the May half term he said, 'I want to be called [name withheld] and I want that name on the register at school.'

I said, 'I know you've asked me if you can be called a boy's name and be a boy at home and I've ignored it and I'm sorry because now I realise how important it is to you. So, let's go for it over the half term and if you feel confident then we can go and speak with your teacher.' So, when he went back, his name was changed; the gender was still the same, but the name changed to a boy's name. We went the whole week using a new name and old pronouns and then he said that we needed to use boy pronouns as it didn't work for him. That first night I went to bed saying to you [looks at dad] in tears that I couldn't do the pronouns. I just couldn't do the pronouns; it was killing me.

People sometimes say it feels like they are losing a child. Again, because I'm trans it's hard for me to properly understand that. What does it feel like, because the change of pronouns, more than the name, seems to symbolise that moment?

Mum: [Looking at dad.] You didn't feel like this, but to me it feels like I've had twins, and I feel a massive sense of loss. It doesn't mean that I don't love my son – I do and I love him more every day – but there is a feeling that he is the stronger twin and the other twin has faded away. That kills me still. [Mum becomes very tearful and we stop for a short time.]

It feels important to have shared that. All our feelings need to be present, and perhaps open, in order to help other people. The gritty bits matter.

Mum: It's hugely important. It's important to meet other people and to share the feelings that others in your situation understand.

Dad: I never felt like that. To me he is our one and only child. The transition just made him happier and I am just so pleased that he is happier. There was a child who was somewhat unhappy who is now happy. There is no loss or negative feelings. I was scared and I pretended it wasn't happening for a time but once I acknowledged it, it was completely positive.

Mum: He really helped me because at the time I was a tangled mass of emotions. I'd dealt with all the logistics – I was the one who'd gone into the school, every day into school I went in and did the hard work. We wrote policies and I was exhausted.

Dad: I didn't have to do much.

Mum: To be honest, I still haven't recovered. I've still not recovered emotionally. He [*looks at dad*] said we had an unhappy child and now we have a happy child. You were my rock when that was happening. I still fall to bits.

When you say 'falling to bits', I feel that it doesn't do justice to the actual work you have done and are doing: going into school, changing and writing policies and raising a child to be safe and happy. You made it possible for me to be here carrying out these interviews. This residential happens partly through the work you do. The work you did in your child's school will have an immense legacy. Can you talk a little about that work?

Mum: So basically, on the Sunday night in half term I honestly thought that he might have forgotten about going into school as himself. I thought that being himself over half term he might have got it out of his system. But at bedtime, when we started to read a story, he said, 'So am I going to go into school tomorrow as myself?' I asked him if that was what he wanted after the half term trial week and he said yes. I said I would contact the head and arrange to go in to talk with them. I knew he wasn't just a tomboy; it was much more. Even before he transitioned, everybody treated him as him.

I remember trying to put him in a dress and it was traumatic for him. It was so deep seated that.

Often when people hear people talking about their trans-identifying children, they say that the children are just exploring gender expression and that it doesn't mean that they are trans or that they need to transition into a different gender; that the parents should just leave them be. But this is different from that. This is much more fundamental. This isn't simply about presentation or expressions of femininity or masculinity but much more about the way that a body and a being in that body are able to be present in life. I quite literally didn't exist until 'I' existed.

Dad: When we did the transition and we informed the school, someone from the nursery who had taught him from an incredibly young age said to us that they knew, and that most of his friends only ever knew him as he is, so the process of transitioning was simple and straightforward for them.

Mum: I wrote a letter to explain.

Dad: Apparently one grandmother read the letter to her grandson and he said, 'That's fine. Boys can marry boys, so it's fine.'

Mum: So, I'd been gearing the school up for his transition and helping them out (he virtually looked like he does now anyway). So, the Monday came, and I waited after school to see the headteacher. We sat there in her office and explained everything. He told her everything in his own words. He was gripping my hand so tight, and in a small voice he said that he wanted to change his name on the register. She replied that they should change his name on his books and his peg, too. His grip released, he relaxed, and it was like he'd grown two inches taller. We started to talk about practicalities, and it was agreed that the next day he would go with his teacher and change his name stickers everywhere they needed to be changed. It felt great. We were very happy.

That was in June, but then in the meeting there was something that still wasn't right. Both myself and the headteacher thought that we would get away with changing his name but leaving his pronouns the same, so he'd still be 'she' at school but with a new name. I could tell that something wasn't right. He said, 'I want to be a boy at school.' There was a pause when no one said anything. His hand started to grip mine again, tight. I said to him, 'Yes, I think we can do that,' but the headteacher was looking at me like, 'Oh my god, I don't think we can handle this.' She said, 'Why don't we do it in September?' His grip on my hand tightened and I knew he wasn't happy. I asked him when he would like to change his name and come into school with the right pronouns, as a boy. He said the next Friday.

The headteacher said again, 'Why don't we aim to have everything changed in September?' But I knew that we couldn't do this in stages, that it needed to happen for his wellbeing in one go – a pronoun that matched his name and gender identity. I said, 'Yes, we will do it as soon as possible, all at once.' His grip released and that Friday he walked into school as himself, confident, not attention-seeking any more, just happy.

* *

Mother of a Seventeen-Year-Old Trans Boy

When and how did your son first come out to you as trans or as his true gender?

Mum: Four years ago. He'd just had his thirteenth birthday. Very unhappy child. We didn't know what was wrong with him. We couldn't work it out. We took him to Paris for his birthday, but he was so unhappy.

A few weeks later he had his long hair cut off.

We tried to integrate him back into school. He'd come out of school because of severe anxiety, but that didn't work. Then he started to dress in a more masculine way – he started wearing boxer shorts. One day in the kitchen, I told him he looked like a lad, and he replied, 'Goal achieved.' I thought, 'Okay, something else is going on here.'

I knew I had an unhappy child full of anxieties, but after he said that I had some idea. I asked him if he'd heard about transgender people and he said, 'Mum, that's me.' That night we had a talk and he showed me lots of research he'd been doing himself and shared lots of information with me. When his dad came home, I said to him, 'Our child's transgender.' He said at that time that he was gender fluid. I didn't know anything about that, so I looked it up to find out more. Since then, he's explained it more to me and told me that although he is male his expression can be either masculine or feminine. I think because he feels like this – fluid – it's taken him more time to adjust.

I wonder if it's him that's taken more time to adjust or that the world around him has not allowed him to be himself?

Mum: Absolutely. And me – if I'm honest – I struggled with the gender fluid thing. I didn't understand it. When I thought he was just going to be male, I thought that was simple, all cut and dried, and straightforward. He kept sending me clips of young people on YouTube who'd had to hide who they were and how depressed it had made them. I thought, 'How have I not known this? How have I not seen this?' But because he's fluid it was harder. He liked wearing dresses, he loved floaty fabrics. But I never put anything down to anything to do with gender.

What's it like to have a child tell you they are trans or gender fluid?

Mum: It's overwhelming. I would look at him and wonder how many years this stuff had been going on in his head. At first, I thought that I could do this because I had answers to his behaviour. He'd been so inward-looking, low and down. He'd walk to the shop with a hoodie up, hiding. As soon as he told me, he'd walk down to the shop with a big smile, almost skipping for the first time like a proper child. It didn't matter to me whatever was going on because it was like I had a happy child, a free child who was not locked into something that I didn't understand.

Did he feel like a child before?

Mum: Before he came out, he was super sensitive and conscious of other people and his surroundings. He found it really hard to make friends. He had friends, but people made friends with him rather than the other way around.

He hated being out; and if he went out, he'd come back home really stressed out. He was an awkward child. The past four years have been a massive learning curve. I struggled with the whole gender fluid thing. I thought, 'If you're male, why are you wearing lipstick some days?' But he was happy like that. But, if I'm honest, I didn't want to have to explain to people that I had a transitioning child, but one that sometimes might look gender confusing. I was worried that people would ask questions. But I get it now: he has feminine qualities.

My mum has struggled recently with my understanding of my 'they-ness' rather than 'she' and 'her'. She wonders why I transitioned if I'm not going to be 'her'.

Mum: When I met other parents of trans kids who said they always knew, I felt quite guilty because I didn't know. It wasn't that straightforward. I know now that I have a child who is going down a different path. I'm sure he would have always been a feminine man had he been born male. He'd never have been a lad's lad. He is the way he is.

What for you has been the learning? You're quite hard on yourself for apparently not knowing about your son before he came out to you. If you heard someone else saying that, what might you say to them?

Mum: I've lived my life in a small box, always doing exactly what was expected of me. I never wanted to be seen but now I think that if he wants to be different, then good. He doesn't care and that has taught me so much about life. I would say to any parent to let their child find themselves and don't be your child's first bully if they tell you. I thought about me being my child's first bully when, after he started to transition, he went out and bought a denim dress and I looked at him and said, 'Why do you want to wear a dress?' He looked absolutely devastated about why I'd said that to him, but at that point I couldn't understand his becoming a boy who wanted to wear a dress. I never forget that look on his face. I thought, 'Why am I so in a box and judging him?'

Why do you think you wanted him or needed him to dress a certain way? Was it being protective?

Mum: Yes, yes. Of course, I wanted him to be safe, I wanted to keep him safe. I'd been picked on over the years. I know how that feels. When we walked down the street, I didn't want people to stare at him. I never want him to be targeted, so I wanted him to conform. But he said to me that he'd rather be bullied or picked on than not be himself, that's how strongly he felt and feels about his identity. I knew I had to support him, however risky it felt for me.

The only way I suppose you can ever truly let someone be safe is to let them be themselves and let them go. What advice might you give to any parent who might be terrified about their child being picked on?

Mum: The only thing I can say is to let them live as their true selves. No matter how flamboyant they might be, you just need to let them do it, even if you are scared they might be picked on. They are being picked on for who they truly are, the bullies can be dealt with. Don't hide and conform like I do. I'm a bit like a robot, a uniform dresser who conforms. I try to look like the other mums. Allow your child to be the way they need to be. My child is so happy now, expressing himself exactly as he wants. He's at art college now and he couldn't be happier.

* *

Trans Man (a Role Model at The Residential Weekend)

Can you just say how old you are and how you identify?

Trans man: I'm twenty-eight years old. I identify as a trans man and I'm here this weekend as a role model.

Can I ask why you volunteer as a role model? I know that giving back to the community in this way is so important, but why is it important to you?

Trans man: I believe that I need to be a role model because when I was growing up I didn't have any support. I didn't even understand any of the words or terminology. I didn't know what it was to be trans. I just felt different and alienated. And it wasn't just small differences; it was loads of differences compared to other people around me. I didn't have any support group to help me through this journey. I just want to be that support for other people. If you don't have the right support, it can be such a detrimental journey. There were so many times when I just wanted to disappear off the face of the earth. I had friends that understood to an extent and I felt a little bit accepted by a small pocket of people, but it wasn't enough. YouTube was my resource.

When did you first know and when did you start to transition?

Trans man: Socially I started to think about transitioning at eighteen – I should say 'externally transitioning'.

I met a friend who was transitioning, and I started to feel enlightened through their journey, just through observation. I knew it was me. I identified exactly with his journey. It wasn't until I was about twenty-one that I started to investigate things more deeply. From my friendship with him I understood more about chest binding and I saw how he approached girls from a man's perspective. I knew that was me too.

I started counselling. Counselling helped me to unpack how I was feeling, but I was still very introverted about coming out as a trans man. It took me until the age of twenty-four to properly socially come out. I followed lots of trans guys' journeys from America on YouTube because I never saw anyone like me transitioning here in the UK. I felt comforted by their stories and in awe of their journeys. I said to myself, 'This is exactly who I am. There is no doubt about it.' I had no expectation that anyone else would understand but internally I knew.

At that time, I took about three months away from everything and went to stay at a friend's house. I told her that I just needed to think things through in almost isolation. I then said to her, "I need to tell you something" and she said, "I know what you are going to tell me."' I'd never told her anything, but she said, 'It's the energy that I get from you and I'd rather call you a boy.' I thought, 'I'm not mad.' It gave me the confidence to come out, so I started to tell family.

I came out to my mum via YouTube. I made a YouTube video. I thought everyone would accept me, but not everyone did. My mum denied me. I so wanted my mum to accept me. When she told me that I wasn't her child anymore and hung up the phone, it tore me in half. I thought, 'I don't have a mum anymore.' I knew she didn't mean it. I knew she'd seen the signs since I'd been young. She felt that I was bringing shame down onto the family – that's a big deal in a Black family. The idea of bringing shame. She could just about handle thinking of me as a lesbian, even though I never identified with being a lesbian.

It's weird how sometimes people can accept you being a 'better wrong' in their eyes, even if that 'better wrong' is not you.

Trans man: Exactly. I remember before I socially transitioned, I was encouraged by a family member to get baptised and join the Church. I tried to detach from my emotions and play into a lifestyle that pleased everyone else. I tried to live a cis-normative lifestyle. It didn't work. I tried to set up a religious group for lesbians because I just didn't know which way to turn. I told a friend that I'd become a Buddhist and explored religion! I think that period made me have a complete breakdown.

To fast forward, after my period in isolation I started to do all the process of transition quickly – I knew it was right. I changed my name by deed poll, changed my documents, started hormones – privately at first as the waiting list was so long. I was still having talking therapy, so I knew I was supported. I did lots of research and documented my process on YouTube so that I could see my emotional changes. I was in and out of relationships, I got a really rounded view of how women felt about me as a trans man who was transitioning. They saw my complete ups and downs. Everything at that time was or could be a trigger for me. I was trying to get to know who I was. I wanted the support of relationships but, really, I knew I needed to be on my own. But romantic security feels important when you are going through it.

Did you always know this when you were much younger – say, the age of some of the young people you are a role model to now?

Trans man: At around ten years old I knew I was attracted to girls, but not as a girl, if that makes sense. I was very close to my dad and we spent hours playing football. In my late teenage years I created an online persona as a guy. They call it 'catfishing' now, but it just allowed me to be me. I would spend hours talking to women online, but it felt wrong and felt empty. So, I stopped but I knew I was transgender. Maybe I didn't know the word, but I knew I was a man. It was never about sexuality but completely about gender.

I didn't hear your role model talk. I wish I had. When you see much younger trans kids, how do you want to help them?

Trans man: Firstly, I think, 'WOW!' The courage they have is amazing. They are looking up to me, but I'm looking up to them. They have the courage that I never had to say how they feel, and then there are the parents who are supporting them and listening, hearing their children. I put the children together with their parents and look at my life and me in the past. I couldn't talk to my parents or express how I felt. I was very introverted and followed a traditional path, a path I'd grown up witnessing. I see these parents come here wanting to support their children and I think they are going to have a much easier life than mine. I feel full of joy and I just share that with them. I'm back in contact with my mum now. I know that deep inside she loves me.

Thank you for sharing.

* *

Trans Siblings

Can you just say how you identify and your ages?

Sibling 1: I'm seventeen and I identify as trans masculine and I use 'he' or 'they' pronouns.

Sibling 2: I'm twenty and I identify as nonbinary.

Can you describe what it is like having a sibling who also identifies as trans; is it supportive?

Sibling 2: It's quite nice having someone who instantly understands what it's like to have to deal with society's expectations of cissexism basically; the fact that society expects you to be one way or the other. When we're out in public, if someone says something, we have each other and we understand.

Sibling 1: It's always been a supportive relationship between us. They were the reason I was able to come out. Because they are older, I felt supported; they have other trans friends. Seeing them express themselves and seeing that my family sort of understood it, if not fully, made it easier for me to identify as me.

Can you go back to that point when you did come out to your family, to the feelings you had?

Sibling 1: It's difficult to remember because I came out a lot of times. I came out to most people individually. I came out to my mum first and then we told our dad. I mainly remember telling my mum. It was difficult. I'm not sure that I was completely ready but if I hadn't done it then, I don't know that I would have. But after I did, my life became so much easier.

How did it become easier?

Sibling 1: I don't remember how I felt in that instant, but I remember the general time after and how good it felt to just be able to live as me.

Sibling 2: I'm not sure I remember you coming out as trans. I remember you coming out as gay – they'd originally come out as a lesbian before that. I remember you coming out as a lesbian. Our rooms are next to one another and one night I heard you crying so I messaged them and asked if everything was alright. They said, 'I don't think so.' I said, 'What's wrong?' They said, 'I don't want to do this over text', so we met up in the bathroom. They said to me that they thought that they were attracted to girls. I said, 'Why are you crying, what's the problem, it's fine.' We went back to bed.

Sibling 1: I remember coming out to mum because she had been out shopping, I was in my room and I think I was quite upset. She asked me, 'What's wrong?' I said, 'I don't think I'm a girl, but I don't know what I am.'

Had you always felt that? I always knew I wasn't a boy, but I didn't really feel like a girl or a woman.

Sibling 1: I remember talking about small stuff to my friends. I always use to stand up to go to the toilet. I talked to my friends and we all tried. I genuinely wanted to. I just thought it was something that all of us wanted to do. I didn't have any problems being called 'she' and people using my previous girl name until I started puberty. Then it really hit me.

Did you notice any of this?

Sibling 2: Some stuff, but it's easy to look back now and understand. I remember their football-crazy period, everything had to be football, and everything had to be in the Arsenal colours. But there wasn't lots of other stuff going on. Back then we didn't know the words or even that gender stuff existed. I knew that they had some issues. I first found a trans community on Tumblr. I knew there was something about the trans community that spoke to me, but I didn't know what it was. I knew I didn't want to make any changes to be a boy. I met other people who were trans and through them I found out that my gender identity isn't the most important thing about me; it's not something that I need to pay lots of attention to. For me, it's much more about my expression of femininity and playing with that. I feel comfortable being nonbinary femme and having the freedom to express femininity in different ways. At first I didn't relate to nonbinary identities because it seemed to be very heavily tied up with masculinity. For me, that transitional aspect of it never applied to me. Nonbinary for me just feels more comfortable to me. I've never felt very binary in relation to male or female. I feel like I have a strong sense of gender identity, but it perhaps doesn't relate to male or female.

I always felt that gender controlling me was always the problem.

Sibling 2: I'm drawn to traditional codes of dress, I like femininity, I think sometimes people find it hard to accept me as a binary-presenting nonbinary person.

Only the word 'trans' works for me and my identity. If you could give any advice to someone that might be in your position, what might you say?

Sibling 2: Don't hold back. Don't try to please anyone but yourself and experiment if that's what you need to do. Meet other people like you. There are lots of communities now, all over, especially on the internet, so link up with them. I've spoken to lots of people who experimented and became part of a trans space, only to find out that they weren't trans. But they needed that safe space to explore and express themselves in. That's completely valid. That experimentation is important; we can play much more with gender.

Sibling 1: I'd say just try and talk to people and listen to their experiences.

If you could change anything in this world, what would it be?

Sibling 1: To have more safe spaces for us – safe gender-neutral spaces. Spaces where you can be yourself and not have to fit other people's standards.

Sibling 2: I just wish that people could be more empathetic.

* *

Trans Girl and Her Mother

What year are you in at school?

Trans girl: I'm in Year 8.

Are you happy at school, do you enjoy school?

Trans girl: Yes, my school is a Stonewall school so it's really LGBT friendly.

Amazing. What's it like to be in a school where you feel supported?

Trans girl: It's okay, the school is LGBT friendly but that doesn't mean that every pupil is. One day a week we have a club called the Equality and Diversity Club. It's really LGBT friendly. Also, if someone in school says 'that's so gay' they get told that it's not funny to say it. People try to make sure that no one who is LGBT is being picked on or having a hard time.

When did you transition at school?

Trans girl: In Year 7.

Was that tough?

Trans girl: It was near the end of Year 7, near the start of the summer holidays.

Can you think back to how you got to the point of being able to go into school as yourself?

Trans girl: I know Mum hates the way I did it, but I posted something on Snapchat about it, I said that I'd always been a girl. When I was growing up, I was a really stereotypical girly girl. I loved Barbies and the colour pink, I loved playing with Littlest Pet Shop.

So, you first posted something on Snapchat. When did you tell your parents?

Mum: I think you told me and Dad first?

Trans girl: No, I did Snapchat first.

Can you remember the timeline of events?

Trans girl: Yes. I was with my friend and we said let's do make-up. And then something in my brain clicked, I thought I've always liked make-up and I've always liked girly things, not that girls have to like girly things, but I did. I'd always felt different. When I was much younger, I'd said to my mum, 'Isn't there surgery people can get if they are born in the wrong body?' So, with my friend doing make-up something clicked in my brain, so I posted this thing. I know it sounds silly and bad but at school I got great support from it. Then I told my mum and dad. My mum said she always knew, and my dad made a funny noise. It took him a little while.

Do you remember the time she told you?

Mum: Yes, very clearly. She had a friend over for a sleepover and they both came trotting down the stairs, stood in the middle of the lounge floor, looking at us and she said, 'Mum, I've got something to tell you, I'm trans, I have a new name, I'm a girl, please call me she from now on and I won't answer to my old name or old pronouns again and there's nothing anyone can do about it.'

Trans girl: Dad made a funny noise again and they paused the film. It was time for thinking time.

Mum: I knew this was coming for a long time because all the signs were there from about four or five years old.

Trans girl: Did you think I would be gay or trans?

Mum: No, not gay but trans. Yes. It was tough on your dad because he felt he had sons. It only took him a short while though.

How did you become strong or confident enough in yourself to post on Snapchat and then go downstairs and say who you were?

Trans girl: I've always been confident. Talking to my parents was like talking to my best friend. It was easy because I knew that they were accepting. I knew that my mum would be brilliant, and she was. In that moment I knew I would hear my mum's voice. Before that I had been through a tougher period, but I'd rather not talk about it apart from that it also took me some time. I remember having a best friend and once someone asked if we were dating and I thought NO WAY, I felt like the opposite to her, best friends.

Does everything make sense in your life now?

Trans girl: Yes, mainly. It doesn't feel like it's falling apart, just coming together. But then some people say that you must have dysphoria to be trans, but I never had it. I never felt dysphoric.

I don't think you have to be depressed, I think if you can be as smiley and happy as you are then that's brilliant.

Trans girl: After announcing it on Snapchat and telling my parents I went into school the next day as myself and everyone knew. I was slightly worried but they all just ran over to me and hugged me. My best friend told all the teachers that I had changed my name and pronoun and that they must get it right. The teachers were brilliant, they just got it right. I stayed in the same school uniform as it was near to the end of term and returned after the summer in a skirt.

Do you feel like more people at school got things right for you than got it wrong?

Trans girl: Yes.

If you could give advice to someone who might be having a tough time, say someone reading your story about having an easier time, is there anything you think you could say to them?

Trans girl: If you're scared about judgement, about being judged, it makes the judgement come to you more impactful. So, if you just say it and say who I truly am, it will make you feel more positive. It doesn't mean it's not scary, but worrying about the judgement and worrying about if you should say or not could just make it worse. It's like getting on a rollercoaster. You could be scared or excited.

I'm in the scared rollercoaster camp. I think some people might not have your support.

Trans girl: My parents and school could have not been accepting but I still would have said it. Maybe it's the person I am. I do feel lucky and I do feel privileged but I'm only being myself so it's not really a privilege.

* *

Trans Teen

Can you remember back to when you first knew or felt that you were a boy?

Trans teen: I always felt very different and I remember when I was a young kid, I felt convinced that I was just a boy. Whenever we played games, I'd always see myself like any other boy. I remember someone telling me that I didn't look like a boy and I really yelled at them. That wasn't like me – I've always been very chilled. The first time I ever put it into words was when I was about thirteen and I read a short story online about a trans guy and I thought this really sounded like me. But I tried to repress it. Then at fourteen I came out to my best friend at the time. It didn't go that well, but they did take it onboard. When I was fifteen, I told my parents.

At that point did you socially transition in school?

Trans teen: I started to socially transition before that, even when people didn't really know. I just passed as male, but I was still using female pronouns. In my school photograph I look like any other boy. But I was still known as a girl.

What was that like?

Trans teen: It was very weird. People who didn't know me just thought I was a boy. I remember the photographer who did the school photographs yelled out, 'Boy on the end, move in.' He was talking to me. It was awkward and embarrassing.

Everyone around me assumed I was a girl. I felt bad. I think I was worried about the situation I might be creating. I felt such a conflict – it was something I really wanted but the people around me didn't know and were confused.

Was school enjoyable for you?

Trans teen: No, I was bullied quite a lot. Often, I didn't know a person and I would only get to know them because they would keep picking on me – sometimes every day. There was one boy who would pretend to have a crush on me as an ongoing joke. It hurt. I always enjoyed learning, so I tried to throw myself into that. But the social part of school was hard.

Did you do well at school?

Trans teen: Yes, I passed my exams. I wish I'd done better but I did well enough to go on to college.

Now?

Trans teen: I'm at university.

There are young people here as young as six and seven who are transitioning and who will go through school as their true selves. How do you feel when you see them?

Trans teen: I'm both really proud of them for being able to discover so early but also kind of jealous that I didn't have the words for that in my time. There are a couple of things that stick in my mind. If someone had told me about stuff like this – trans stuff – and I didn't just think that the awful time I was having was normal, then I would have been able to be one of those children.

Me and my friend have known each other for literally our whole lives and just by chance we are both trans. We think that if we hadn't known each other and made each other feel okay, then we might have realised far sooner that we were trans. We didn't need a word for it. We were just being ourselves. Even if the world seemed to not understand, we did. We used each other to register what was normal.

Thank god you did have each other to alleviate some of the tougher bullying. Are you happy now?

Trans teen: I'm way happier than I ever thought I could be. I had top surgery a few weeks ago, which has given me so much freedom. Before, I'd never leave the house without a binder on, and at university I'd rarely go to the shared kitchen to get food because I couldn't face putting my binder on. I'd hide away. Now I feel that I can do so much more. Beyond dysphoria I just feel so much freedom to have a body that feels like it's mine. Wearing a binder is incredibly hot and sometimes it feels hard to breathe.

You look very happy. There's such a brightness and openness to your face. Happiness is radiating outwards.

Trans teen: Thank you. Before in my life I felt like a character from *The Sims* – like I was robotic, like I wasn't a real person.

What was it like to try and live like a character from The Sims?

Trans teen: It just feels like a huge blank. I felt like I was controlled by what I was supposed to do and not what I wanted to do inside.

I don't have many memories before I transitioned – certainly not happy memories. Looking back, they don't feel like my memories.

Trans teen: I have the exact same thing.

Are you doing what you want to do now at university and in your life?

Trans teen: Yes, I am. My family is very academic, but I have gone into the creative world. I feel like I'm really in control of my life now.

Who have been the people who have helped you through this?

Trans teen: Both parents are supportive, but my mum has been there all the time. My dad works away a lot, so for most of the stuff at school and to do with my GP, Mum has been there throughout. My mum has been good at knowing my rights and supporting me with doctors.

If you could imagine going back to talk with you at twelve or thirteen years old when you're not so happy, when you're living life like a character from The Sims, what would you say to you?

Trans teen: I'd tell them not to give in to any feelings of doubt and to try and find a community. I'd tell them not to feel scared.

* *

Trans Teen

Hi, can you just tell me how old you are and how you identify?

Trans teen: I'm seventeen and I identify as a girl.

Are you still at school?

Trans teen: No, I left school last year and started an apprenticeship at an IT company that I previously did work experience for.

What do you do?

Trans teen: I work as an engineer, helping people with their IT issues and setting up systems, et cetera.

I'm terrified of technology, so that instantly sounds incredibly impressive. Was that what you always wanted to do after school?

Trans teen: When I was at school, I didn't really know what I wanted to do but I'd always planned to go on and do my A Levels and go to university and perhaps study Computer Science. When I did my work experience at this company, they offered me the chance to stay on and do an apprenticeship. I thought I would take it to get out of school and do something different.

Did you like being at school?

Trans teen: I found it quite difficult when I realised I was trans. I found it difficult to be at school because I didn't feel it was a place where I could be myself.

How old were you when you realised you were trans?

Trans teen: I was fifteen and I started to do stuff about it almost as soon as I realised. As soon as I worked up the courage to tell my family – in particular my mother – we started doing things and she was really helpful. The night I told her, I gave her this letter (I'd spent weeks, maybe months, writing it) and asked her to read it in her bedroom. She came into me and just expressed how much support she would have for me, whatever. This was just after reading the letter. The next day she was already talking to her doctor about me and about referrals to any services I might need.

What was it like to have that positive response?

Trans teen: I was surprised. I was so unsure about how it would go but I knew I had to tell her, so there was no point in holding it from her, however it went.

What had school been like before that point?

Trans teen: It was quite uneventful. I never had many friends. I found it quite difficult to relate to other people at school, so I just got my head down and got on with the work. I used work as something to focus on.

Before fifteen, had you any idea about the way you felt?

Trans teen: I didn't know that people like me existed. I had never heard the word 'transgender'. I think if I'd known about it before – knowing that people are transgender – then I might have realised earlier. If you don't see yourself, you don't feel like you can exist. The first time I read about people like me was on the internet and I thought, 'What if that is me?'

What was that feeling like, to think, 'What if that's me?'

Trans teen: It was a scary feeling. I didn't want this thing about me to dictate how the rest of my life would go but I also knew that I couldn't ignore it.

What did your mum's positive response mean to you at fifteen and what does it mean for you now, two years on?

Trans teen: At the time it was such a relief. I knew that she would always stand by me and that if we could get through this, we could get through anything. Two years on, I feel like it's allowed me to really know what I want to do with my life. Maybe it is feeling safe?

Have the past two years been smooth? Maybe that's what your mum's brilliant response allowed for?

Trans teen: I don't have to think about being trans most of the time, which I really like because I just want to get on with my life. Because of her support, I feel like I can get on and do that. With regards to my transition, I'm feeling okay.

Do you have a plan for how you see that transition being or playing out in the future? It feels like you don't see yourself as being trans, rather just like any other seventeen-year-old girl going out into the world and approaching womanhood. How does trans fit into that or does it matter?

Trans teen: I think it shouldn't matter. I think for me specifically it doesn't matter. I just want to get on with my life and finishing my transition as soon as possible will allow me to do that.

Do you, or could you, see yourself as a role model?

Trans teen: There's nothing spectacular or extraordinary about my life that would make me a role model.

There is something spectacular about making your life feel comfortable for you to exist in. That's a huge thing. You're doing it brilliantly – never underplay that! It's people like you who will change the world.

Where do you see your life in the future? What are your hopes for your future?

Trans teen: It's still something I'm trying to figure out, I'm not sure where I want to be. I want to progress in my career. I just want to be happy really and not full of worries. New experiences make me happy. Being able to go to work as myself is brilliant but it's normal now. It became normal quickly.

If people are where you were, perhaps two years ago, what might you say to reassure them?

Trans teen: I would say that people will be better than you think they will be about it. While being trans might be the centre of your life, it won't be the centre of theirs. It's just one thing about you amongst many.

Trans Teen's Mother

One of the things that came up when I was interviewing your daughter was about writing the letter. She talked about how your response to the letter enabled her to move on. What was that moment like for you?

Mum: It was a huge shock. It was very emotional. I was crying as I got to the end of the letter. I'd only had a couple of little hints before that in the previous months. I didn't know anything about transgender stuff at all. Reading the letter, lots of stuff started to come together. She was brushing her teeth the next morning before school and I just went up and hugged her and said it was alright. We cried and hugged. She told me her name, which she'd already chosen; and being my daughter, she had of course read and learnt everything that there is to know. She is an IT genius! Then I had to learn everything – the last page of the letter was information and support groups.

What is it like to be the mother of a child who must be going through such distress but who still also has the space to create an information page for you at the end of the letter? It's such an act of generosity.

Mum: It was amazing, but it didn't surprise me because that's how she is. It's how we are – we're detail people. Ridiculously so. The resources she provided were useful and helped me out afterwards, but in the moment I was overwhelmed with emotion, feeling sad but happy. The happy thing was starting to come in because my fiancé and I had always wondered what was going on with her. We had huge behaviour issues. I thought it was down to me being a single parent. I really struggled because it felt like she needed so much from me. She was never naughty but she always had to argue back and never allowed me a moment to think. I ended up being such a tired single mum with a really quiet child who didn't want to spend time with other kids.

How was she at school?

Mum: I spoke to the school and asked them to keep an eye on her but I think she was just a bit of a loner, playing on the outside. So, when we found out from the letter, so much of the past made sense. I'd got to the point of having counselling to see what more I could do.

You said you'd had a couple of hints before the letter?

Mum: Yes. One time we were in a bookshop and normally she would never even look at books as she's into her phones and iPads. I was looking at some cookery books and I noticed she was looking at a book and reading it. She looked quite interested in it. She said she wanted to get it and I wanted to encourage her to read, so I bought it. She quickly showed me the back, but I didn't really look as I didn't want to be nosey about what she was reading as she was nearly sixteen. When we got home, she read it all in one day. It was a fairly big novel. Monday, when she was at school, I was doing something in her room and I had a quick look at the book. It was about a trans kid coming out at school. At the time I thought that maybe it was just a teenage thing and I didn't think too much about it. I didn't jump to any conclusions. I never mentioned it to her or anybody. A while later we were creating emojis – emojis that look like you, ones you use to represent you when you send different things. So, she's really techy and helped her not-so-techy mum to create her emoji. She did mine and then hers. She did hers as a girl. I thought, 'Is she mucking about?' I didn't say anything. I didn't know anything about trans stuff at all. Unless you've come across it or know someone who is trans, then how do you know about it? So those were the two little things that came up.

Thinking about them retrospectively, they weren't small things.

Mum: Yes, once you know. It was probably only a couple of weeks later that she gave me the letter. It was about nine o'clock at night and she was brushing her teeth and getting her things ready for school the next morning. She said, 'I want to give you this.' I thought it was probably a school newsletter but as soon as I started to read it, I could tell it had a serious, 'Dear Mum', tone. I've only read it twice, and quite quickly. When we talked about it the next day, it wasn't for hours; it was maybe twenty or thirty minutes. She gave me the letter on a Thursday night. I was so pleased to finally know what was going on for my child and why she'd been so down all the time. We still fight a little like cat and dog though!

The energy it will have taken her to manage feeling different would have been enormous and she's still seventeen. She said she had spent months thinking about and writing the letter. It must have taken so much out of her. What differences have you seen in her?

Mum: I think she's dealt with the trans stuff, the transition, brilliantly. I think we all have. We're all doers. It's been tough as the doctors wouldn't give us any support, so we've had to go privately. Luckily, financially we're able to do that. We have flown along.

We've gone through the first clothes shopping trip together. We had a cry in the changing rooms together. I wanted to keep it together for her and we were trying to keep it down because of the other people changing in the other cubicles. But it was lovely, and it feels so long ago. Now when we go shopping, we try on loads of things and she'll say, 'Don't look, Mum.'

When you think about her future now, what do you see as a happy future, a happy place for her?

Mum: I think I have to guess where her happy place might be. We're not at the place where we talk about that kind of stuff. She's a teenager and I'm not the person she'd often talk to about those things. I think we're too close. I love it now that she's got other people to talk to. She knows I'm always here to talk to. I'm just so glad though that now she is being herself. From day one I've been incredibly happy about that. It's ace that she is being who she wants to be. All I care about is her being happy in herself and in whatever she is doing.

She's doing so well at work. We've always known that she would do well. When she was two, her talking and writing were so good; she's always been so accurate. My mum was a proofreader and I think it's come down through her. When my daughter was little, we used to play these games every single night where before bedtime I'd write a message for her on a small white board and draw a picture. Messages like 'Tomorrow is whacky Wednesday' or 'Thursday is terrific Thursday'. We did it for years every night so that she woke up to it.

If you could give advice to anyone around trans stuff, what might you say?

Mum: I would just say take every day as it comes as there are so many different emotions to go through. You have to go through the bad emotions to come back up to the good feelings. Let your child be who they really are and not hold back from any support for them.

What is it like to be the parent of a trans child?

Mum: To be honest, I don't think much about it now. I'm the kind of parent who might overreact to lots of little things but I did lots of reading to try to get my head around everything. I remember the first weekend I found out I went out for a walk – just me and the dog. I found a place to sit and I just cried and cried. The next day I could see that she was able to be herself for the first time.

* *

Trans Girl (Aged Eight)

Can you tell me what year you are in at school?

Trans girl: I'm in Year 3.

Do you have a favourite lesson or lessons?

Trans girl: Probably PE or Art. PE in the summer [*hesitates*] and Art in the summer.

Do you have a sport you like most?

Trans girl: Swimming.

Is that the sport you are best at?

Trans girl: Yes. I can only swim fifteen metres though.

That's quite a long way. What would be your favourite thing to do in an Art lesson?

Trans girl: Pointillism.

Can you explain what that is?

Trans girl: It's where you draw a picture and you colour it in, but you don't use strokes, you use dots. In Art we drew one by ourselves and then we had to copy one.

What was your own drawing of?

Trans girl: A mythical tree.

What does a mythical tree look like?

Trans girl: My friend drew one with a ruby in the trunk, but I didn't. I drew all my leaves going downwards, but no ruby.

No ruby?

Trans girl: No. But the colours aren't just brown and green, they collide with each other.

In Art is it okay to paint a tree any colour?

Trans girl: Yes. I distort the colours.

Do you enjoy being at school?

Trans girl: Yes, because we do fun stuff. I enjoy the fun stuff more than the essential subjects.

If you could have any superpower, what might it be?

Trans girl: Freezing time, so I could walk around while everything is frozen. Actually, no, I want to change my superpower. I want to be able to erase memory.

Whose memory would you erase, or what memories?

Trans girl: I wouldn't erase all your memories, just a single part of the memories. I would erase bad memories. And sad memories and angry memories. Like my memories from camping when I got three cuts. Two have healed and one is healing.

Has school always been a happy place for you?

Trans girl: Not really, but I don't want to talk about it.

Do you have any ideas about what you might want to do when you grow up?

Trans girl: Be a YouTuber. I'd make videos about robots that I'd change every fortnight, and videos about stick fights, and eating outdated food ones.

Do people really make videos about outdated food?

Trans girl: I don't know but if I do, they might copy me.

Could you do that as a job?

Trans girl: It is a job! But at the start, if I don't get enough money, I'll get a part-time job as a janitor or cashier or work at a fast food restaurant.

Trans Girl's Father

You're the first dad I've got to talk to today. It was the same at the last interview session. Do you have any idea why that might be?

Dad: Yes. I think it's largely because women, mums, embrace this much more openly and tend to want to get ahead of their children's feelings and provide care. My wife is far more organised than I am, and she did all the research immediately when she realised what was happening. She found the support and connected us to other people going through the same stuff. Then she educated me, and then as a team we worked out how to move forward.

When you first found out, what were your feelings?

Dad: To be honest, I think at first I was getting over myself and my own preconceived feelings. What would people think if we were walking down the street? How is this going to impact her as she grows up? Is changing her gender the right thing to do? I think there were a lot of those doubts at first. My father was incredibly supportive and both he and my wife said the needs of the child must come before your own feelings. I realised that I had to get over myself and do what was best for her. There was an initial resistance from me because of my mindset.

Was there an immediate emotional response, and what emotion was it?

Dad: Yes, I think it was largely fear.

Where does that fear come from?

Dad: I think it's largely to do with the evidence around me as I was growing up. A whole set of preconceived references that were based in fear around what would or might happen to her. Just a set of stuff in your brain that you must get over.

Was that an easy thing to get over?

Dad: No. I'd probably say at least a couple of months of thinking and discussing it with other people before I could embrace it.

If you could give advice to any other fathers or parents who might be at that fear stage, what might you say?

Dad: I think the only thing I would say is that it's not about you, it is only about the child. Whatever or wherever they end up, it is their life and not yours, so try to let go of the baggage that prevents you from being there and caring. Try to embrace and focus on your child's best interests. The other thing is, the first time, for example, that you walk down the street with your child as they want and need to be, the world doesn't notice. Your fears can be unfounded. They just see a little girl happy with her father. On the odd occasion where a friend you haven't seen for a time says, 'What's going on? Why is your son wearing a dress?', you just must explain it in simple, straightforward terms. It's never as bad or as hard as you imagine. They just accept the words from their friend.

Most of the situations that build up in your head are never as bad as you imagine. The first time those things happen, those first questions (we call them the 'slap-in-the-face' questions), you can just say, 'We don't have the answer.' You don't need to answer. My child became as happy as anything to be herself.

How proud are you of her?

Dad: Her courage in being who she is, is wonderful. She has no baggage, so little fear. She is also super resilient. When things have been slightly awkward, she tends to shrug it off.

Do you have any fears about the future?

Dad: Yes. Coming together with other parents of trans children, especially teenagers who experience problems, I worry about how she might deal with the stuff that life throws at her. But her being informed and us getting ahead of it to provide support allows us to follow her as she tells us what path she needs to follow. We understand far more now about her potential future routes. We'll embrace the fears and worries as they come.

* *

Mother of a Trans Daughter (Aged Almost Ten)

When was the first time you heard the word 'trans'?

Mum: I don't know, I knew trans people existed and I had a friend who I think would identify as trans, maybe fluid. I didn't know any other trans people. But I knew what it was.

Can you remember the day, or the week, perhaps the month, when trans as a very real thing came into your life?

Mum: Kind of. I remember I'd been posting photographs of my kids on Facebook and out of the blue an old friend of mine sent me a message saying, 'I hope you don't mind me saying this, but have you ever considered that your child is trans?' She explained that her stepdaughter is trans. I was a bit shocked and in myself a bit defensive. I thought, 'No, that isn't what is happening.' I thought, 'I just have a kid who rocks a dress, who is gender whatever.' I wasn't bothered. I think by that point she had started to say stuff, but I had a younger child who was two and she was at that time only four and I was separating from their dad. Everything was full on, so when she said stuff like, 'Don't say "brother" say "sister"', I didn't think about it too much. Looking back, I thought, 'Whatever, it doesn't mean anything.' I just rolled with it. But she was very definite about it. She started to say, 'Don't say "he", say "she"', and I thought, 'Yes okay, but let's get your shoes on for school.' Then trans as a concept – in that she might be trans – started to come into my life. After that, it appeared really clearly one night when she was crying her eyes out in bed. I said, 'What's wrong?' and she said, 'I mustn't grow up into a man. I don't want to have a beard.'

How old was she then?

Mum: She was four.

What's that like to have a four-year-old be so distraught and tell you that the remedy for their pain is potentially so far out of your comfort zone?

Mum: I was shocked. I was listening to her and I felt such sadness because she was so distressed. But it was very clear to me what she was saying. There was nothing vague. There had been a build-up of different signs: for two years she'd never wear trousers; the pronoun stuff; the 'sister not brother' stuff. I was like, 'Okay I get it now.' But I was shocked at our reality.

What did you do after that shock?

Mum: There was a period of maybe a month or two when the same thing would happen every night and we would talk. She said she wanted to be a mother, to have babies, to not get a man's voice or body. Then after that it all happened quite quickly. She'd only ever wear girls' clothes.

To school?

Mum: Yes (she'd already worn girls' clothes to nursery). She refused to wear any boys' clothes, including swimming trunks and underwear. We'd sometimes be out – in shops for example – and I'd be calling her and people would look round and think, 'Where is this boy you're calling?' I could see people wondering why I'd given her a boy's name. The look on their faces. We started to have a few questions. We went to a festival and this kid asked, 'Are you a boy or are you a girl?' Everyone was confused because she still had a boy's name. She said she wanted to pick a girl's name and start using it. To be honest it made perfect sense because her old boy's name was just causing confusion. Then about six weeks later she changed her name to a girl's name. She was adamant that this was now who she was and that nothing would change, and it hasn't.

It all sounds very organic and almost easy. She was so young, so that must have helped. But did you face any problems from school or those around you?

Mum: When she changed her name, I sent an email to everyone. It was a total zero tolerance email that said: 'This is how it is. We are really glad that she has told us. We are behind her. Please be completely onboard or just don't be in our lives. There will be no tolerance for misgendering or asking her questions. If you have questions, ask me.' That felt like the big deal. People didn't really question us. We did have a little uniform issue at school which has been sorted out. I did meet with the headteacher about the uniform and toilets.

Did you have any support at this time? Did you know any other parents of trans kids?

Mum: No, I didn't really have any support. I had contacted the local LGBT group for support with the school. They were really good and came into school with me. Then I found Mermaids and they really helped. It helped knowing that there was support out there, but it was a while before I met other trans kids or parents of trans kids.

How was she coping at that time?

Mum: She was fine, absolutely no problems. The problems came later as she realised that she was different. At the time she just wore the clothes she wanted to wear, changed her name and she was oblivious to the fear that was going on in me.

What was that fear?

Mum: I didn't want her life to be hard. She had some additional needs and I was worried about her future. But she was happy and not aware of my feelings.

How is it now?

Mum: She is just pre-puberty and has started at primary school. She's been at two schools. At the first she was completely in stealth and no one knew her; only the head and her class teacher knew. At her new school a few people know her and knew her before, but no one talks about anything, which is what she wants. The school is quite good; they've done some work around it.

Does the word 'trans' matter in this conversation?

Mum: We didn't use that word for a long time. She's aware of what that word means now and about other trans people.

Do you wish she wasn't?

Mum: No, I think now she's almost ten it's important because we've had to start talking about things such as puberty. Partly because she's been questioning what will happen, I don't want this man stuff to happen. I've had to say to her that when that happens there is medication she can take to stop that from happening, so now she is aware of what hormone blockers are. She's seen a psychologist a couple of times so that she can get a report to enable the process.

Knowing your child and knowing her journey, what would it be like for her to go through a male puberty?

Mum: It would be horrific. [*Cries. We take a break.*] There is no way that is going to happen, unless, of course, she changes her mind. I don't think she will, but if she did, I'd support her. But as a parent I am not going to take a risk with my child.

To those people who question you as a parent thinking about giving your child hormone blockers, what would you say or what do you think?

Mum: I think she has had it relatively easy. She's had great support, but let's be honest, it would be much easier for her to live her life as a boy. She could easily slip back in – she has 50 per cent boys as friends and 50 per cent girls, and she likes football and stuff. It's not been easy for her to stand up to people and she lives in fear of people finding out. That's not an easy life. Why would anyone choose that unless there was no other way? If she is that definite from four years old, then we must follow her. When she was eight, we had a conversation about changing her name and gender marker on her passport. We emphasised that this was a huge step and asked her if she was sure. She said she could change back if she wanted to. She can stop hormone blockers. I'm pretty sure that she will be leading the way.

It doesn't sound like you are making the decisions. What's it like to be a parent of a child who has such a definite plan for their life which is entirely different to the way you imagined it would be?

Mum: It's total surrender. A lot of my parenting life is not how I thought it would be. Having a child who, apart from being trans, has a disability (for the want of a better word), has impacted all our lives: school, where we live, my life. All our life choices have been shaped by her needs. That's just the way it is.

I've found a way to follow her determination but also allowing for her to change, stop or adjust stuff. Who knows if she'll change her mind. I've had to find a way to follow. On the one hand, I feel like I don't quite know her yet but on the other hand, I feel like our connection is so deep because we have connected on a soul level. But I'm aware of our identity difference. I've had to let go of control.

If you could offer any advice to anyone else in the same or similar position you were in a few years back when this came into your life, what would it be?

Mum: Just listen. All that stuff about it maybe being a phase... I guess the less you do and the less you interfere, the more likely it is that their true self will unfold. If it is a phase, then the more likely it is to play itself out. If it's not a phase, if that is their true self emerging, then just listening helps them to come out. Also, total acceptance has given her the confidence to express who she is and, in some sense, if she changes her mind, she knows that she will always have total acceptance.

So, you're not invested in her becoming anything but her best self, you have no bias. It sounds like pure parenting where you just create the environment for growth and safety.

Mum: For me her confidence in being herself and living her life is all that matters.

* *

Trans Teen

How old are you?

Trans teen: I'm fifteen.

Are you still at school?

Trans teen: Yes.

Do you have a favourite subject at school?

Trans teen: Drama. I love Drama.

Why Drama?

Trans teen: Because you can be someone else. I've always loved Drama for that reason. I don't know if I'm any good at it but I just enjoy it.

Are you happy at school?

Trans teen: I am now but I wasn't in the past. I've moved school four times.

Can you tell me a bit about why you weren't happy? You don't need to go into any detail you don't feel comfortable with.

Trans teen: The environment of the other schools was different. The schools didn't really understand or support LGBT issues. They just didn't get it or me.

When did you come out as yourself at school?

Trans teen: About two and a half years ago, at the end of Year 8.

Can you remember the first day?

Trans teen: Yes. I cut my hair and went into school wearing pants (trousers).

What was that like?

Trans teen: Scary.

Was there a lot of planning or preparation?

Trans teen: I cut my hair to raise money for charity, but the other reason was for me to express myself. There was about six months between changing the way I looked and telling people about me. I started to look masculine though before anyone knew.

What was it like before that point, not being able tell people your truth?

Trans teen: Hard. Really hard. I had to do PE with the girls and get changed with the girls. That was one of the main reasons I left that school.

There are many people who talk about trans people using bathrooms and changing rooms. Can you say what it was like for you to have to use the girls' changing rooms when you had already started to socially transition into your boyhood?

Trans teen: It was so uncomfortable. I didn't feel comfortable using the girls' changing room or the boys' at that point. Using the boys' facilities made me feel scared. I was afraid that they would find out and the stuff that happened in my old school might happen again.

It breaks my heart that you would feel scared. When you felt like that, what happened to your learning at school? What impact did it have on your schoolwork?

Trans teen: An awful lot. I got that down about it because they were giving me death threats and saying that if I went into school again, they would kill me. They made a group chat called 'Tranny onboard'. They used to say, 'You're a girl and a minger.' It got to the point where I got so depressed that I made several suicide attempts and I ended up on an inpatient unit for six months.

I know this might seem like a strange question but when you were going through that awful time did you have any dreams and hopes for your future?

Trans teen: Yes, I thought about becoming an animal inspector and looking after animals. That's the future I want.

What was it like to see your school time being eaten up by the awful time you were having to go through?

Trans teen: I suppose I got used to it. I accepted it and tried to put on a front. I let them walk all over me. I tried to stop them.

What was the front that you tried to put on?

Trans teen: I tried to pretend I was fine and coping and that no one needed to worry about me.

Can we talk about the better place you are in now? How did you get to this place?

Trans teen: I got private treatment, which really helped. I'm on hormones – testosterone, which I've been on now for six months.

What difference has that made to your sense of wellbeing?

Trans teen: A lot. My body shape and my voice have changed. My face has also changed. I feel much safer. I'm also on hormone blockers so that I don't go through a girl's puberty, which has helped. I've also moved school, which is a lot better and a lot more accepting. It's a good school. Only a few people there knew me before.

There are some people who say that people under a certain age shouldn't get hormones or blockers. What would you say to them to let them know the difference it's made to your school life?

Trans teen: I don't think I would have made it to sixteen if I hadn't got them. That's the impact it has. People don't listen to us, but we know our own minds.

Who has helped you the most?

Trans teen: My mum and my little brother. My mum has been there for me when no one else has. She really stood up for me. She's always there. She's taken me shopping for clothes. She bought me a binder and a packer, which have really helped me to overcome my dysphoria. She also bought me shaving cream!

Have you shaved yet?

Trans teen: No, not yet.

Where are you happiest?

Trans teen: With people that understand me and allow me to make them happy.

Are you happy in school now?

Trans teen: Yes.

How is your schoolwork coming on?

Trans teen: My schoolwork is still a bit behind, but I am getting there. I was out of the system for a time and I moved school a few times. I'm not good with change.

I'm not sure many of us would be good with that much change. What does it feel like to have lost that time at school because of the bullying? What would you say to the bullies?

Trans teen: They must be insecure as they look for any little thing they can pick on – someone wearing glasses or someone being trans.

If you could give any advice to someone in your position or in the position you were in a couple of years ago, what might you say?

Trans teen: Be yourself, and life is worth living even if it doesn't feel like it is now. You'll always be the person you are meant to be: a boy or a girl. Eventually everything – the inside and the outside – will match up.

Is that happening for you? Is everything matching up?

Trans teen: It is, slowly, but it is.

Trans Teen's Mother

What was it like for you as a parent to hear your son talk like that?

Mum: It was quite difficult. He left out some of the more extreme stuff, maybe because he's in a much better place now. I think it's hard for him to go back to how bleak things have been.

How bleak were they for you as a parent?

Mum: There were times he didn't want to live. He's made several attempts to take his own life over the last couple of years and there were times when he didn't see a future. So, to hear him now talking about the future in a genuine way makes me so happy. He has put on a front before, but I could tell he was trying to be positive for everyone else but not for him. I could tell today it was for him.

How powerless do you feel as a parent when all this stuff is happening around your child?

Mum: What you want to do as a parent is protect them. Sometimes you want to step into their shoes and fight for them. There were times when no matter what I could do, it wasn't enough. I had to become a bystander. I did feel helpless.

How can you become empowered in that situation of feeling helpless?

Mum: By learning and educating yourself, meeting other people and being supported by a network which means that you're not alone. You're not a lone voice. Being informed helps you to stand your ground. But most importantly for me, when I listened to him and what he (my child) needed, I was able to be his voice. There were times when he wasn't being listened to and what he was saying was being dismissed, often by people saying 'That's not a big deal' when it was a huge deal. Things like him being misgendered, people telling him he couldn't use the boys' toilets. That sort of thing. People saw those as tiny things, but they were huge, life-and-death things. So, by being informed it meant that I could stand up for him and say, 'No, you're breaking the Equality Act.'

How did you become informed and empowered to help his journey? Are there examples you can give?

Mum: When they don't see something happening, they think that it's not happening. There were, and still are, a lot of processes and decisions going on behind the scenes that he wasn't aware of. He assumed that no one was listening. One of the things that really helps is to let him know the step-by-step processes that are happening. I am often the go-between and it has really helped his journey for me to be open and transparent.

Around trans lives there is often silence and people saying they don't understand you or your journey. There are lots of times when trans people are trying alone to navigate an incredibly complex space whilst dealing with the emotions that are bubbling up.

Mum: In his new school he has a great head of house who works with us as part of the team. There was a teacher in his school who was continuing to misgender him, but within a day it was addressed and dealt with. Both of us were fully involved in a transparent process. It gives him faith in the adults around him. He realises that they have got his back. It makes a vast difference to his school life. Out of school he is in the Cadets and there he has a great sergeant. She really has his back and listens and acts. He had an incident when they were doing water sports and he needed to get changed out of his wetsuit. He was hanging around waiting for the accessible toilet to become available. (They just had group changing facilities, either all male or all female, and showers that were completely open. Clearly, he couldn't get showered with the girls or the boys.) He was waiting for the accessible toilet to become free, and a member of staff was like, 'What's going on here, get in the shower.' So, he had to out himself and say that he was trans in front of whoever was there. He had to out himself. He was there in stealth because he just wanted to be there as himself. The sergeant raised the issue as high as it needed to go to implement training and new protocols.

How proud are you of your child to know that he has found a way through this often difficult maze to be himself, and how angry are you about the stuff he has gone through?

Mum: It makes me really pissed off. If that had happened six months ago, he would have left the Cadets. It probably would have ended in another overdose; it would have resulted in him staying overnight on the children's ward and maybe becoming an inpatient again. But it hasn't this time, I'm so proud of him for getting through it. Being outed is a huge thing.

What are the best things about being the parent of a trans child? What are the bonuses?

Mum: The bonuses are getting to see him flourish. He's in a place now where his mental health is really starting to improve. We are getting the support we need now. Seeing him take a delight in his animal care, I see a future for him, and he sees a future. This time last year it was very dodgy but it's not now. Now there is hope and I cling on to that hope. I still don't feel that I can let my guard down as I'm always having to fight, but there is now a sense of normality.

If you could give advice to someone who might be in that awful moment when they don't know if their child is going to make it, is there any advice you could give?

Mum: I would say make sure you get a support network around you. You don't need to do this alone. There are people who have been through that exact process who are coming out the other side now. Hold on to them, hold on to that hope.

On the darkest days, how important was your support network?

Mum: Exceptionally important. Especially when you are surrounded by naysayers and people who don't get it, you have to find and cherish the people who do get it.

* *

Mother of Two Young Children (One Trans and The Other Gender Fluid)

You said you have two children?

Mum: I have three altogether. One who is eight years old and defines as trans (male to female) and one who is just thirteen who has very recently come out and said that they feel more comfortable describing themselves as gender fluid. They are questioning lots and going through a process.

What age was the younger child when they told you?

Mum: They were about five.

Do you remember the moment?

Mum: Yes, I do. I was doing the ironing and she came in, sat in the corner quietly and started crying.

I said, 'What's the matter?'

She said she didn't know if she could tell me.

I said, 'You can tell me anything.' I thought she might say that she fancied boys.

She said, 'I feel really confused and I don't know if I can tell you.'

I said, 'I'm your mum and it's my job to make sure you are happy and safe. If you feel like you can tell me, then tell me. If not, then you can tell me another time.'

She said, 'Mum, it's really weird. I've got this boy's body but in my heart I'm a girl.'

That was how she told me.

What was it like to hear those words?

Mum: I had this rush, a rush that came up from my toes and overwhelmed me. You know in films when it's all slow motion? It was a little like that, but then I knew that my child was in front of me crying so I immediately picked her up and gave her a cuddle, saying, 'It's alright. If this is what you are feeling, then I'll look after you. If that's how you feel, then that's how you feel. That's who you are.' I hid the fact that I went into turmoil straight away.

What were the feelings beneath that turmoil?

Mum: I just felt as if someone had switched off the light and hit me. It was a stunned 'What the hell?' It was nothing I expected. We live in such a small place that I was terrified about the reaction. I didn't sleep. I spoke to my then husband and he had real problems getting his head around it. I could tell from my daughter's words that she knew who she was. She was a girl. She said, 'In my heart I'm a girl.' She was five.

I walked away in shock. I learnt a lot about myself. It was nothing I'd ever thought about or prepared for.

What did you learn about yourself?

Mum: I learned that I wasn't as open-minded as I thought I was, which was hard because I'd always felt like I was a supporter and an ally and that I would stand up for anybody. But then when my child told me, it hit me. Fear hit me. Fear for my child. But also, from a selfish point of view you have your dreams of how you imagine your child's life will go. You have an idea of a dreamy path they might take. I thought I didn't know my child at all.

To those people who feel that parents might be pushing their children towards being trans, what would you say?

Mum: Absolutely ridiculous. It's the complete opposite of that. I couldn't even think or didn't even think about having a trans child. It never entered my head. She always wanted to dress up and wear dresses, she always drew amazing eyelashes on with my eye liner. If anything, I thought she'd grow up to be a great drag queen. But nowhere in my mind did I even think or consider the word 'trans'. The worry I started to have about keeping my trans child safe went to a different level.

What were the things that helped you get from fear and worry to where you are now?

Mum: Connecting with other parents. I researched like there was no tomorrow. I knew I had to support my child and I needed to find out how to do it best. I had to get over the guilt as a parent. I had to stop questioning if I was doing it right or doing the right thing. I kept thinking, 'Should I be doing this or that?' I questioned my parenting even though I knew deep down I was doing the right thing. I just wanted to nurture. I spoke to some very close friends who were very supportive. I spoke to my mum and we grieved together and then supported each other.

When you grieved, what were you grieving for?

Mum: I don't know. I have no idea. I just felt this massive sense of loss. He was my boy and he was such a lovely boy. He was quite fabulous. At that time, I felt like I was losing him. Now I can see that I wasn't losing him; he is still there but he was always she. She was always there. I will go on to have a fabulous daughter, another fabulous daughter.

A while ago you talked about having dreams for your child. Do you have a plan now for your daughter?

Mum: No. She will do whatever she wants. She will become whatever she wants. She will lead and I will follow. That's it.

In a way she always did lead.

Mum: Absolutely.

Are you scared about her growing up?

Mum: No. I think by truly being herself she'll develop the confidence to live her life. She has blossomed. She's doing so well in school now. Before, she was struggling and getting so behind. She's got friends. She's so happy.

* *

Trans Girl

Can you tell me how old you are and what year you are in at school?

Trans girl: I'm six and I'm in Year 2.

Do you have a favourite lesson at school?

Trans girl: Art.

What is your favourite thing to do in Art?

Trans girl: That's a hard question. I think painting.

Do you work from your imagination or paint things that are around you?

Trans girl: We do all of those things.

Are you happy being at school?

Trans girl: Yes.

What makes you happy about being at school?

Trans girl: I can't answer that question, it's too hard. It's much too hard.

Have you always liked school?

Trans girl: Yes. When I grow up, I want to be an Art teacher.

Are you enjoying being here this weekend?

Trans girl: Yes, I like all of it. I like seeing all the other people. It makes me happy.

Trans Girl's Mother

Your daughter uses very few words to sum up how she's feeling. She talked about being happy. Is that how it is?

Mum: I wouldn't say so. She's really good at putting on a front. She's very good at hiding how she is feeling. I've realised since she transitioned how much she keeps hidden. When she said to you about feeling happy at school, I think that's only partially true. I think she does really like school, but she goes through a hell of a lot at school. She gets an awful lot of stick but she doesn't let on.

I think I understand as I was that kid, but no child should have to keep that much in. It must be so hard on them.

Mum: She withholds a hell of a lot that she never tells me.

When or how did you find out about her identity?

Mum: When she was six, earlier this year. She started to tell me that she felt like a girl. I just said 'Okay' and then carried on with what I was doing. I didn't want to make a big deal out of it. Then she started to say it more frequently. Then she told me that she wanted to change her name and that she had decided on her new name in the playground with her friend. But at the time she would only let certain people call her by that name. I asked her if she wanted me to let other people know and she said, no, she'd prefer to let people know. It was a confusing time as some people were calling her one name and other people were calling her by her old name. Within three weeks of her first mentioning it to me, she'd socially transitioned at school. She told all of her teachers she was a girl, told me we needed to change her uniform and then marched into school, confidently, as herself.

What was that like for you?

Mum: I think for the whole of the first week I was on the phone to the Mermaids helpline asking for help. I just talked it out. I didn't know what to do. I just wanted to do the right thing by her, that's all you care about. I just needed pointing in the right direction.

What's it like as a parent to not know the right direction?

Mum: The team at Mermaids brilliantly told me to just follow her lead. That was scary but it really helped. I would advise anyone to take each day as it comes. Let them lead.

It must be tough when your six-year-old says this is what needs to happen for me to be happy.

Mum: It is, but every step she's taken has made her happier.

She even said that we should take her old clothes to the charity shop. I didn't. I put them in the loft just in case she changes her mind. I don't think she ever will.

What is it like being the parent of a trans child?

Mum: I do worry about her, about her future, but I hope the world becomes a kinder place. Being a parent of a trans child isn't a thing. I love her, whatever. I would never change that, whatever is thrown at us.

* *

Trans Teen

Where or when are you happiest?

Trans teen: I don't know if there's a 'where' but I'm happiest when I'm with people who understand me. I love my family. I love being outside, in the middle of a forest for example.

Why do you feel happy with these people?

Trans teen: Because I feel safe with them. It's easy to not feel safe when you're different.

What does it feel like to not feel safe?

Trans teen: It feels like you're alone in the world. Usually when I don't feel safe it's because no one I feel safe with is around me. It makes me feel alone.

When did you first know that you might be trans or that your assigned gender didn't fit?

Trans teen: I think I was eleven or twelve. I was starting secondary school. I went to a very religious Jewish school where the uniform was very strict, so girls had to wear skirts and boys had to wear trousers. So, I had to wear a skirt for five years of school. The minute I had to put it on when I started at secondary school was the worst moment of my life and every day going to school was a struggle because I knew that people would see *skirt* and see *girl* and I knew that *wasn't me*.

Can you explain how that felt?

Trans teen: I wanted to tell everyone but I didn't want to tell everyone because I didn't want to be that other. I didn't want to admit to myself who I was because I was scared of it.

What were you scared of?

Trans teen: Scared of people leaving me. Scared of the looks that people might give me. When you tell people your truth, the way that they look at you changes and it's hard to get that back. The thought that my family might not look at me the same way. Thank god that didn't happen, but there was that fear.

How did you move from that moment of fear to where you are now?

Trans teen: I told my sister, about a year before I came out to everyone, that I knew that I was a boy. I knew she'd always support me. I wanted to tell her first, even though I knew I had an incredibly loving and supportive family. I knew it would be harder for my parents. I knew my sister's view of me would never change.

How old were you when you told her?

Trans teen: I was fifteen. My sister had a friend at school who was trans and who had socially transitioned at school. I didn't know anyone who was trans, but my second week at school back in Year 7 I went up to him and asked if we could talk sometime. He said, 'Yes, just come and find me after lunch.' I never went to find him because I was scared. I knew I was a boy, but I had no idea what trans was.

How did you know?

Trans teen: Everything. Just a feeling. How does anyone know? By how comfortable you feel? I was never comfortable. I had a stereotypical boy's childhood: I played football; I went to sports things with my dad; all my friends were boys; I wore boys' clothes; and if ever I had to wear a dress, I'd cry. If anyone gave me anything pink, I wouldn't want it. I was always a stereotypical tomboy, or boy, but then as puberty happened it changed. Before then I never knew that there was anything that separated me from the other boys. Puberty happened and I had to wear a skirt and there was something visually different between me and the other boys. That hurt. I thought, 'I'm not the same as them anymore, but I want to be.' I didn't understand what was going on.

How did you tell your family?

Trans teen: First, I want to say how amazing my family is. I feel like I'd be dead without them. When I came out to my mum, if she'd said anything different than what she did say I'm not sure what would have happened. The situation felt fragile. Even the people I was most scared to tell have been brilliant. My grandma has been wonderful, my uncle who has always been so macho reacted brilliantly. He said he'd always known.

I came out at a family dinner. The waitress was calling me 'she' and my family were calling me by my birth name because they didn't know. I started shaking and crying and went outside and sat on a bench. My mum came out after me and I told her. We cried and we hugged, and she told me she loved me and would come on the journey with me. She has. She comes to Pride every year and supports me in every way. I named myself after the restaurant!

Where is your life at now?

Trans teen: I'm in my first year at Sixth Form doing my A Levels. I have two part-time jobs.

What are your A Levels?

Trans teen: Photography, Psychology and Drama.

Have you got an idea what you want to do with your life or career?

Trans teen: I want to go into film making. I want to create stuff. But short term I'm going to take a gap year. I'd like to look into war photography.

Is there anything that you think you can't do because you're trans?

Trans teen: It's quite tough not being outed, like in my part-time jobs going forward as I don't know how people would react. One of my part-time jobs is as a delivery driver at a chicken shop and I wouldn't know how they might react.

They think I'm cis and straight. I know passing is a horrible concept to people who think it shouldn't matter, but to me it's safety and I don't want people to see me as trans. I just wish I'd been born a boy; my life would have been so much easier. I know it's different for everyone. The trans community is such a wonderful blessing – like the people I've met here, but I still don't want to identify as trans.

Would you ever give any advice to anyone? What if you could talk to the you back in Year 7?

Trans teen: I don't know. I think I'd say just keep going, I'm not going to say that it will definitely get better, because sometimes it doesn't. I know that's not what we're supposed to say, because people don't want to hear that, but I would say that there is the possibility that it could get better and that possibility is sometimes enough.

* *

Interviews: Part 2

These interviews were carried out with young trans and non-binary people in a series of Saturday afternoon youth sessions with Gendered Intelligence.

Trans Girl

Can I ask how old you are and what pronouns you use?

Trans girl: I'm eleven and my pronouns are 'she' and 'her'.

Have you always been this fabulously confident?

Trans girl: Yep.

If you could talk to someone who is also eleven and trans and struggling to find their confidence, what advice might you give them?

Trans girl: Just sing it out. When I sing, I feel happy, proud and excited about my life. I can't really describe it, but it's a really strong feeling inside.

You're doing a great job of describing it. Is being trans a happy place for you?

Trans girl: Yeah.

Same here. What have been the things that have helped you be this happy?

Trans girl: My mum. She's been a really big support.

How have school been?

Trans girl: Yeah, they've been great. We have a really great assistant head in our school and she's been great, really helpful.

If you could talk to other teachers, headteachers and assistant headteachers in other schools, perhaps where trans pupils are having a tough time, what would you say?

Trans girl: I would say, 'Hi, I'm trans and I don't think you are being helpful AT ALL. You need to get your "A game" on.'

Sometimes I speak with young people in schools who are having a really tough time because the staff don't have their 'A game' on and perhaps don't understand or believe the young person when they talk about their gender. What would you say to them if you had the chance?

Trans girl: I would say, 'You're wrong, you're DEFINITELY wrong. Everyone knows their own minds even if they don't know anything else. Even five-year-olds, they know what they're thinking inside and you don't, especially without your "A game" attitude on.'

How old were you when you definitely knew your own mind?

Trans girl: I was five years old.

Did you tell people when you were five?

Trans girl: No, I waited until I was nine. I waited four years.

Can you remember those years of waiting before you told anyone? How did you feel in those years?

Trans girl: I still felt pretty happy but now I feel double or triple that happiness.

What's it like to be living your life now? What's the first thing you think about when you wake up?

Trans girl: Cupcakes and rainbows.

And your last thought at night?

Trans girl: The bright moon shining making a beautiful essence across the sky.

If you could reach out and speak out to other young trans people, what would you say?

Trans girl: You're perfect just the way you are.

* *

Trans Teen

Do you come to this group regularly and why is it important to you?

Trans teen: I started coming to GI [Gendered Intelligence] groups about a year ago. I've only been to this one a couple of times as I usually go to the older group. It's very different to other places. Here I can use whatever name I am using at the time and whatever pronoun I want. People use the names and titles you want and it's like you can let out a breath you've been holding in for ages.

What's it like to hold a breath in?

Trans teen: It's kind of like I don't notice holding it in unless it's a bad time or something bad happens. But it's like you don't notice how much stuff you're carrying around until you breathe out and you can just stop.

How long have you felt like you have been doing that?

Trans teen: A long time. A really long time.

Did you feel like you were carrying all this stuff through your school years and holding your breath?

Trans teen: It was exhausting. Really exhausting. My school was incredibly gendered. Girls and boys had separate PE tops and the girls' tops didn't have buttons but big, deep

V-necks. Girls had to wear skirts like old-fashioned tennis players wore.

Other people wouldn't notice those things. If you could talk to other people to let them know what it was like, what would you say?

Trans teen: I think before I knew stuff about myself, I didn't think about the small everyday things that were making me unhappy. Only after I knew more about me did I understand. It almost made me feel worse because I knew why. Things made sense, so I could put them into a context – the supposedly little things like the shape of a neckline. I realised that for years I'd put up with so much stuff that for me felt wrong, like the gendered clothing and people thinking I was someone I wasn't. I'd been down on myself for so long that knowing it wasn't my fault allowed me to breathe.

What would you say to schools to allow it to be a little easier for us trans folk?

Trans teen: Please try not to gender divide – like separate boys' lines and girls' lines. Have private changing options that respect all of us – trans or anyone. Not many people felt comfortable getting changed together. Respect us more and listen.

Did you do well at school academically?

Trans teen: Yes, I got good grades but I never enjoyed my school years at all. I only had a very few people I could share my suffering with. But we never talked on a deeper level about how stuff was making us feel. I had a few close friends who are still friends now.

What are you doing now you've left school?

Trans teen: I'm just trying to figure everything out; trying to make sense of it. My future seems too big to think about now. I need to just understand me now.

If you could give advice to you seven years ago, what advice would you give?

Trans teen: Just because other people have positions of power and authority over you doesn't mean that they know more than you do about you and what you need and what will make you happy. Only you know that.

* *

Trans Teen

Can you tell me your age and the pronouns you use?

Trans teen: I'm nineteen years old and I use 'she' and 'her' pronouns.

When did you come out?

Trans teen: I came out twice, or many times in a way. I came out to my friends in February last year. They all thought I was trans, but I was in denial and described myself as gay.

What was it like before you came out and what is it like now?

Trans teen: It was a really weird and confusing time. I must be honest and say that I wasn't sure what 'transgender' meant or was. Actually, I didn't even really know what 'gender' meant. When I came here, I had loads of realisations about myself. I knew I was trans. I told my parents and they said they'd rather have a happy daughter than an upset son. I'm much happier now. I just enjoy being me more. I like the way I fit into society now, the clothes I can wear, the image I can have, the way all that makes me feel. Maybe I'll have surgery, maybe not. Who cares? I'm still me and I'm still trans.

What does coming to a space like this mean to you and your happiness?

Trans teen: Oh my goodness... I can't think of a word for it... Yes, I can: 'hope'. Hope for me, hope for society, hope for young trans people like me. It's a really safe space. You can be having an awful time outside or in school and you come here, share your name and pronoun and then just relax, join in or go and sit in a quiet space; speak to other young trans people who understand; see friends or mentors or youth workers; be with people I can look up to and people who can look up to me. It feels like a small community.

Like a family?

Trans teen: Yes, but of friends. A brilliant trans-only space.

When you think about people who haven't accessed spaces like this for one reason or another, what would you say to them?

Trans teen: Don't give up. Have hope. See if there is a trans youth group near to you and try to get to it. Be your true self and try to find people who will just accept you without question.

What do you want to do with your future?

Trans teen: Modelling. I definitely want to be a model and also maybe do some youth work with a group like GI [Gendered Intelligence]. Even though I identify as a binary woman, I want people to see how different I am as that. Not everyone needs to look the same, even if they identify the same. Modelling would allow me to do that, to be my own kind of woman.

* *

Trans Teen

Is this the first time you have come to this group or perhaps any trans youth group?

Trans teen: Yes, it's my first time. This is the first trans youth group I have found, and I was really looking forward to coming. It's been good so far.

Is this the first chance you've had to spend time with other trans people your age?

Trans teen: Yes, it is. I didn't know any trans people before. I'd never even talked to another trans person.

Can you explain what that feels like: to not know anyone else that you can identify with?

Trans teen: It's really frustrating. You know there are people like you because you hear about them and you see them online, but knowing that you haven't met anyone in person makes you feel that it isn't true and that you are the only one, even though you're not.

What's it like to feel like you are the only one, even when you know that you're not?

Trans teen: It's hard because I couldn't tell anyone because they wouldn't understand what it's like; they're not trans. Even your parents, even if they are helpful and supportive, they don't understand what it's like to be trans. You're left with yourself.

When you feel alone, how do you manage to self-care, to get up, to be happy, to get to school?

Trans teen: I manage to get into school because I know an education will help me to be happy in the future. I want to do a job that makes me happy.

Do you know what job?

Trans teen: Yes, I want to be a pilot. I'm already doing training. Sometimes it is hard to get out of bed in the morning and face your problems, but I know it wouldn't help just to stay in bed.

What are the main problems you face? Is it the reactions of others?

Trans teen: Not really. It's facing the things that I see as problems, but they seem silly in my head, so I wouldn't tell anyone. I don't know why the problems become silly inside, but I don't tell anyone apart from my family, who completely support me.

When did you tell your family?

Trans teen: About six months ago. It took me a long time to tell them, I felt like I didn't have the guts, even though I thought they would accept me because they'd always said, 'We will love you whatever.' I also worried about telling them in case that isn't me when I'm older but I realised that if it isn't me then I can just change things. But it is the only way I feel happy.

Exploration is fine.

Trans teen: I was worried that people might judge me if I change my mind.

It's a huge decision, but you are being the best person you can be today and that's all any of us can do.

Trans teen: I wish people wouldn't make it such a big deal. I wish it could be more fluid. It shouldn't be a big deal. If people stopped making 'trans' such a big decision, it would have made my decision easier and more valid because I was constantly worried about changing my mind. It took me a long time to feel this happy in myself and to accept that if I change my mind, then that's okay.

If you could speak to someone out there who feels alone and perhaps hasn't found other trans people to meet or mix with in this kind of space, what might you say?

Trans teen: Stay true to what you think and feel inside, even when it's hard to believe in yourself. Try and make sense of how you are feeling but trust in yourself and definitely find a group so that you're not alone. Most people you will be around are not trans and finding other trans people makes you feel not alone.

When did you start wanting to be a pilot?

Trans teen: Since I was really young. My dad's in the RAF so I've always been around planes and the military. I started my training two years ago now with a disabled flying charity and I fly small aeroplanes. That's really helped me through all of this. Sometimes when you're trans you can become so caught up in your own problems that you lose interest in things. Learning to fly has kept me going. It's helped me through this tough time.

* *

Trans Teen Friends

Is this the first time you have been to this group?

Friend 1: No.

Friend 2: I've been to the other one but not this big one.

Friend 1: We normally go to the other one for our age group.

Is it an older group or younger?

Friend 1: It is aimed at our ages: eleven to fifteen.

Why is it important for you both to come to this or the other group?

Friend 2: I come because I really can't be out anywhere else. This is the only space I can be open in.

Friend 1: It's nice to be with people who understand you, often you are the only one, like in school.

What's it like to feel that you are the only one?

Friend 1: It's hard because people don't understand. Normally they think you are a bit weird or they are overly sympathetic to you, which makes you feel that you are different to everyone else and that you need pity.

What's it like for you to not be out anywhere?

Friend 2: No one is that open about trans stuff, not my family or my friends. My school doesn't have a good way of dealing with it. I'm only out to one or two friends. It's hard sometimes, but I suppose I'm used to it now. I try to ignore the way I feel.

Does coming here help?

Friend 2: It helps a lot. I can open up a little bit here. I don't really like to talk about personal stuff. Drawing helps – it calms me down.

Are you a talented artist?

Friend 2: Some people say I am.

Friend 1: You are!

Is that what you might want to do later after school at college or university?

Friend 2: No. Probably I'd like to do Computer Science.

The way you spoke it sounded like you were out to more people.

Friend 1: Yeah, I started coming out to my friends just over a year ago. I told the more accepting ones first and then the others after. I told my parents just under a year ago and I got my name changed on the school register a few months ago.

You have a fabulous name.

Friend 2: It's a legendary name.

What was it like for you to tell people, what were the feelings?

Friend 1: It was quite hard. I think my mum knew already, or sort of knew because she looked around my phone a lot. It was harder for my dad and he didn't want to call me by my new name. He said he didn't like change, but he's come around now.

There are people out there who say that young people don't know their own minds. What would you say to them about how it feels to hide?

Friend 1: It's really hard. Every time someone uses the wrong name or pronoun it hurts, and you want to tell them that it's not you, they're not seeing you, but you can't.

And now that you don't have to hide, your smile has grown to the size of your face!

Friend 2: Your smile is so big!

Friend 1: I feel that people know and accept me as a boy. I get to wear rock star make-up and rock it. It all makes me so happy to be seen.

If you could both give advice to someone out there who feels that they are the only one, what practical things could you say?

Friend 1: Just remember that you're not alone, you're not weird. Just hang in there because things will get better, they will.

Friend 2: Just think about someone who you might be able to come out to, even if it's just one person. If you can't, it will get better, it is getting better for me.

* *

Young Trans Man

Can you tell me your age and the pronouns you use?

Trans man: Yes, I'm twenty-three years old and I use 'he' and 'him' pronouns.

Can you talk a little about how you came out?

Trans man: Yes, I came out at nineteen. I'd been gender questioning for about a year before that.

What were the responses?

Trans man: Overall it was quite positive. I'm quite stubborn, so if someone didn't want to accept me, I moved on. My family were quite positive.

When we were talking about self-care before in the whole group, you talked a lot about the importance of pronouns and being misgendered. How does it feel when people address you wrongly?

Trans man: With me a lot of it is wrapped up with passing. Before I felt I passed as the gender that I identify with, if I was misgendered it hurt and was uncomfortable. But I feel I could cope a lot better with it then than I would if I was misgendered now. We are still at the stage where people see what they want to see. People don't yet show respect to how someone identifies. Before, when I looked very feminine, I would get misgendered all the time. I worked in hospitality and I got misgendered all the time there. I got used to it. But if it came from people who knew, then it really hurt; misgendering does.

When you say you got used to it, what does it feel like to have to get used to it? For people who say that misgendering is a small, inconsequential thing, can you explain what it feels like?

Trans man: It feels awful. Your chest goes tight inside and you feel like you can't breathe. Sometimes you want to say something, but you worry about someone's reaction. Will saying something put you in a dangerous situation? It's awful having to spend your days asking people not to misgender you.

What's it like not to be misgendered, to be addressed correctly and respectfully?

Trans man: The only way I can explain it is to say that it's euphoric – completely and utterly euphoric. The first time I had someone use the correct pronouns towards me, I felt like I was buzzing. The first time someone called me handsome, the first time someone said, 'He's over there', I could feel myself buzzing.

People outside of our world often see pronouns as a tiny thing. Can you explain why being called handsome is not a tiny thing?

Trans man: Because for however long in your life – maybe years, maybe half your life – you have been wrongly labelled and called by the wrong name and pronoun, to have someone address you properly without question, without a scientific interview beforehand about why you are using different pronouns, just allows for ease and simplicity.

Why do you think people struggle?

Trans man: Because it makes them uncomfortable, I think.

Why would your happiness make anyone feel uncomfortable?

Trans man: Who knows? There are people out there who don't identify as trans but who struggle to fit into a gender binary, and people make them feel uncomfortable. People often worry more about getting the gender of pets right than they do about us.

How did you look after yourself when you were being misgendered throughout those years?

Trans man: Sometimes it became overwhelming, so I'd remove myself from that situation. I'd go to family and friends who knew and who I knew I could trust. It helped to have a few trans friends.

If you could give any advice to someone who might be being misgendered all the time or a lot of the time, what might you say?

Trans man: No matter what anyone says, you know yourself better than anybody else does. Regardless of what anyone else sees, you know what you feel in yourself. Don't allow anyone else to try to change how you believe in yourself.

I watched you constantly reach out to support others in the group. How did you become this solid and generous?

Trans man: I had years of tough times, being misgendered constantly, and it made me stubborn or determined to get through.

How did you remain kind throughout those years?

Trans man: I saw older trans people who'd come through the tough years and I saw a life I could have. I looked up to them and maybe I want to be a role model to others now.

If you could say something to those young people who might read this and look up to you, what would it be?

Trans man: Let me think about it... [*Pause.*] Regardless of how you identify, you are valid as you, and thousands of us will stand behind you like an army and we will protect you.

* *

Trans Teen

Why is coming to this group important for you?

Trans teen: Because it lets me know that I'm not the only person like me in the world. It makes me feel less alone.

When you're not here, is it easy to feel like you are the only trans person in the world and how does that feel?

Trans teen: Yes, and it feels horrible. I feel like I have to lead a double life: one where I hide and one when I'm happy and open.

What would it be like to be able to be yourself all the time?

Trans teen: It would feel great. It would be really nice to be out everywhere.

What do you want to do later in your life?

Trans teen: I want to sing and I also have a business idea which is a fashion shop by day and a lesbian bar at night because we need more lesbian spaces. I will have a button that changes the till into a bar. I might still sell clothes and other merchandise at night-time, but it becomes a bar – a place where people can relax. It might also have a hairdresser's in it. Also, I can sing there as it's my shop and my idea.

Great idea! In that one place do you feel like you could be you?

Trans teen: Yes, I'm going to buy the whole building and then I'll feel like I can be me and help other people – other trans people – feel safe there.

* *

Trans Teen

Why is this space important for you?

Trans teen: In my day-to-day life I am the only trans person I know and see. I get loads of questions and people not under-standing me. I get bullied a lot, so outside of here it's not easy to authentically be me. Everyone here understands me, and I can relate to them.

What's it like when people ask you questions all the time?

Trans teen: It feels really invalidating. Occasionally, people are being really mean but most of the time they are just being curious, asking kind of uneducated questions. So, I'm not sure it's really their fault, but it's embarrassing and invalidating even if they feel like they are validating me. It feels like I'm constantly having to prove and convince people that I am valid and that I am who I am.

What are your feelings about going to school if you have to face these questions?

Trans teen: Well, I do enjoy school because I love learning and I enjoy revising. I'm probably not great at socialising and being with lots of people, especially because there is a separation between me and them because I am the only trans person. It's really isolating.

What would you want to say to those people who ask you intrusive questions and what could schools do to help you to feel less isolated?

Here you're incredibly sociable, so you're not anti-social, so I wonder if the questions make it easier to be alone and away from it?

Trans teen: Schools could definitely have more education on what being trans is and means. Part of the problem is that the questions I get asked are sometimes from my teachers or other grown-ups. Surely, they should know that some questions shouldn't be asked because they are inappropriate.

How did you come out at school?

Trans teen: I asked them to change my name on the register and told my closest friends. My school is big and to be honest I'm probably quite irrelevant in the grand scheme of things in the school, so lots of people always ignored me. Now more people are asking questions because of the stuff they see in the media. Some people try to get my pronouns right and some people don't, and my identity seems to make them feel really uncomfortable. The media is horrible to trans people, so they pick stuff up from there.

What is it like to be young and see the media coverage of trans people around you, especially when you are at school?

Trans teen: It's really scary. You can constantly see in newspapers and on social media people saying transphobic stuff, lots of casual transphobia, making jokes or even saying violent stuff. Trans voices get lost in the amount of transphobia there is. I feel like saying, 'We're just humans trying to get on with our lives and be respected. Leave us alone.'

I'm incredibly sorry that you have to be exposed to that level of transphobia.

Trans teen: With the media thing it's really frustrating because people come to me, the 'trans person', with so many misconceptions and silly questions about what being trans is. I'm the only out trans kid in a school of a few thousand pupils.

That's a big school. What does it feel like to be the one out trans person?

Trans teen: It's scary. Because of the media there are people who think I'm scary or creepy. People sometimes bully me in the bathroom. They can be violent. I just want to come and learn and be a student; that's all I'm there for.

What would you like to say to the adults who are writing transphobic stuff in the media that creates so many misconceptions which you at fourteen are having to deal with? If they were sitting next to you now, what would you say to them?

Trans teen: Educate yourself and please have some respect. There is literally no reason to spread all these lies about us. These horrible stories turn a whole bunch of people against me, a fourteen-year-old trans kid trying to go to school. I don't really talk about being trans at school because it's not relevant. Here it is, but there – at school – I just want to learn. I just want to focus in Physics.

Coming here must be so important to you.

Trans teen: This is a space where I feel safe and can be here without being challenged. It's safe.

If someone reads this and feels like they are the only one out in their school or area (maybe they are the only one), what would you want to say to them?

Trans teen: Stay strong. You have a community. Go online and find trans people, trans people your own age, and try and find a place in your community. There are people like you.

Do you know what you would like to do with your life as you grow up?

Trans teen: I definitely want to work with animals, so I'm really just trying to focus on my science subjects now.

* *

Trans Teen

Can I ask you when you first came out to people?

Trans teen: I did my coming out this past summer holiday – to my friends, first of all. It went terribly. My friends were really transphobic; they were homophobic too. When I told them I was gay, they said, 'That's not okay, you can't like girls', and I said, 'I don't like girls. I'm gay, I like males.' I had to explain to them that I identify as transgender and as male. One of my friends said that her religion was against it. I know her religion isn't against it; it's a personal choice. I know other people who are religious who are gay or lesbian, so it's not the religion.

What does it feel like to be courageous enough to tell people and then have to face negative responses?

Trans teen: I've been hiding being transgender for around seven years. For the first few years I was in denial and, in a way, I tried to treat it like it wasn't a big deal. But then as time goes on and people use the wrong name and pronoun, it just feels like the world is being rude to you. They're not really, they just don't know. It feels really lonely. It has sometimes felt like the whole world is staring you down. When I came out to people, I really thought it would be easier. It still feels like there is a door between me and the world. It's difficult to talk through the door. It's shown me a tough side to the world. Maybe I'll become tougher as a result. It certainly hurts less now when someone is transphobic. When I'm here, I feel under the rainbow and part of a huge community which opened its arms to me and defended me.

What does being under that rainbow feel like? As you said it, your face lit up.

Trans teen: It feels like you have a family that you'll always belong to. It feels like sunshine, like you are finally feeling the warm rays of being alive. Once you can tell people who you really are, even if it goes negatively, it's like the fog is lifting. It's like they know who I am now. It feels like I'm me and no one can take me down. Just watch me.

I feel inspired listening to you talk. If you could talk to you seven years ago, or someone in your position seven years ago, what advice might you give them?

Trans teen: I'd say definitely try not to hide. I know that sounds scary, and if you are in a non-safe space, one that might be transphobic or homophobic, think of a safe way to come out; but if you feel like your surroundings might be safe, think about who you could come out to – a friend or maybe a counsellor or a youth worker. Being alone can make you feel very dark. I felt suicidal sometimes because I felt so alone. I want to include a **trigger warning**.

Okay, thank you for saying.

Trans teen: I did attempt suicide a few times. If you need to hide, like I felt I did, then at the same time try to find at least one or two people you could safely come out to; it really changes the way you feel, it lets light in. If you really can't tell someone in person, then maybe think about connecting with transgender youth groups online or by phone. Creating a transgender family is so important to feeling comfortable. Comfort matters. Just think about whoever you want or need to be, whoever that is, is who you are.

In terms of self-care, do you think that connecting with other young trans and nonbinary people is important or maybe even vital?

Trans teen: Yes. Putting yourself first is also important – thinking about your needs. You need to like and love yourself. I've always been rejected in relationships and I've never been in love with someone else, so I'm not sure I can give advice about that; but trying to accept and love yourself is so important.

You have a whole lifetime to find someone and fall in love if that's something you want or need.

In those seven years when you felt you had to hide your identity, how did that impact or affect your education?

Trans teen: It ruined it. From Year 7 to Year 11 it was really hard, I was at an all-girls school, often alone in a corner, not feeling that I could come out as a boy in that environment. It was so hard. At the end of the last term before the school holiday I spoke with the school counsellor, which helped. I think that would be good advice if your school has a counsellor.

* *

Final Interview:
Pansy

The final interview in this book is an imaginary interview between me now and the eight-year-old me, Pansy. The Pansy who quite brilliantly came out at school in 1972 and then was forced back into a closet by a world not ready for a trans kid to be happy.

This interview is imagined but based entirely upon the facts of one summer term in 1972. I'm now a fifty-five-year-old trans person who likes 'they'/'them' pronouns although the world still constantly uses 'she'/'her' with me because at one point I did use 'she'/'her' and I look like a stereotypical version of a 'she'/'her', so it makes sense to a binary world to address me in that way. Bless them!

I am a writer and incredibly happy. I have a lovely house I never thought I'd have, a group of adorable friends – both transgender and cis – and two wonderful dogs who pull me in different directions when we go for a walk.

I want to talk to my eight-year-old self whilst they are completely happy in that single summer term in 1972 when they asked most of the school to call them Pansy and 'she'/'her'. This interview takes place 47 years ago.

Trans Girl (Pansy)

Can I first ask you your age and the pronouns you like to use?

Pansy: I'm eight years old and I'm not really sure what a pronoun is.

A pronoun is what the world uses to sort you out into either being labelled as a boy or a girl. [This is 1972 so we haven't quite realised that there are many other options, including 'they'/'them'.]

Pansy: Well, the easiest way for me to answer the question about pronouns is to say that I hate being put in the boys' line. There are lines for everything in my school, and the lines are always boys' lines and girls' lines. I feel horrible in the boys' lines. I hate having to use the boys' toilets and I hate being laughed at for wanting to be in the other line, the line that makes sense.

Have you always felt like that?

Pansy: Yes. As soon as I knew the words 'boy' and 'girl' and knew that they meant different everything, I started to feel uncomfortable. Not uncomfortable in my body but uncomfortable in the world. I didn't ever feel like a boy, even though when I looked in the mirror, I saw what the world was seeing: a boy. But inside I never felt like a boy. I have two brothers, one younger and one older, and they both like being boys. They enjoy it, I can tell. All I feel is uncomfortable and like nothing really fits me. I watch my sister and she is my role model. I want to be just like her because I feel just like her.

Can you explain that a little?

Pansy: Well, all the things I'm expected to do aren't the things I feel comfortable doing. Like, I'm expected to grow up and become a man and maybe become a father – a dad like my dad. But that feels uncomfortable and makes me sad just thinking about it, whereas when I think about maybe becoming a mother – like my mum – I just feel happy and warm. It makes me smile. It feels like the stuff that makes me smile also makes the world mad at me. The world bullies me for the stuff that makes me happy. That's confusing.

Do you know the word 'transgender'? [I forgot it's 1972 and that word isn't used like it is now.]

Pansy: Nope, never heard of it.

When you asked people to call you Pansy, what did you say to them?

Pansy: I said that I was just like the other girls and that the name they were using didn't feel right and that calling me

Pansy and treating me like a girl feels right. It makes me happy about coming into school.

Are you happy in school?

Pansy: I am now. I know that some of the other children in the school laugh at me, and I know that some of them call me a pansy rather than Pansy, but I don't care because for the first time I feel like I can run around and be happy like the rest of them. I've only ever been friends with other girls and I never thought there was anything odd or strange about it, but I heard people sometimes saying that it was strange and that I was a sissy or a poof. On one of my school reports it said that I seem to prefer the company of girls and not boys and that I should be encouraged to be more boisterous and outgoing (whatever that means). I'm happy to look after the guinea pigs at break time and make daisy chains. I don't know why that isn't 'outgoing' enough if it makes me happy. Who am I hurting?

No one.
   You were very brave to ask the other children to call you Pansy. Did it feel brave?

Pansy: No, they were already calling me 'a pansy', so I just changed it so that it suited me and not them. It wasn't bravery; it just let me feel happier, especially when my teacher started to allow me to be called Pansy during carpet time and story time on the carpet. I would spend the whole day looking forward to the time on the carpet. I never have a single day off school. When I grow up, I want to write a story like *James and the Giant Peach*. That's my favourite story. I dream about floating away in a peach with a group of strange animals who all look after each other.

Are there other things you learn about in school that you like?

Pansy: I like looking at maps of the world. We have a round globe in our classroom and sometimes if I'm in the classroom on my own I play a game of spin the globe. I spin the globe, close my eyes and touch my finger on the world as it spins and make it stop; and where my finger is, is where I go, to get away from here, to be happy. Then what I do is write a story about getting there and about the people I meet.

Where have you been so far?

Pansy: To tell the honest truth I cheat a little bit. I peek. I open my eyes slightly so that my finger lands on certain places I want. Once, before I started to slightly cheat, I put my finger on a place called Siberia. Afterwards, when I looked it up in the book about different countries, I knew that some things couldn't be left to chance! Now my finger always lands on the sunny places like America.

My dad loves cowboy films, but they only really feature men as cowboys and very few women, who are normally in frilly dresses and who always seem unhappy. But I imagine becoming a happy cowgirl who rides a horse across the mountains in sunny America just like the men in the film.

Does your dad, or anyone in your family, call you Pansy and treat you like a girl?

Pansy: No, they all just see me as a sensitive, quiet boy. I haven't told them yet. I'm not sure when I will. My dad worries that I'm too girly anyway. I've heard him talking quietly to my mum about how my not playing football or liking to play fight is strange and that I need to toughen up; how I should learn to fight and stand up to people. I'm plucking up the courage to tell him. I think I'll wait until the holidays and tell them then. Maybe he'll realise how tough I am then.

What does it feel like when people call you by your other name and by the pronouns 'he' or 'him'?

Pansy: It makes me feel like I'm nothing, empty. I can see them make the shape of that boy's name or the words 'he' or 'him', and I can see the words coming towards me, but they don't reach me. Instead they fall to the floor in front of me and end up in a big heap of 'Simons' and 'he' and 'him'. Wasted words. I feel sad for Simon because he doesn't really exist; he only exists if I pretend he does. Like when I try to walk like a cowboy to please my dad.

Does it please him?

Pansy: I don't think he notices. He only notices when I fall over because my toes turn inwards. I'm pigeon-toed. People tell me that I'm the clumsiest person in the world and I think,

'No, I'm a cowgirl riding my horse across the mountains in America, but you can't see me. You only see a clumsy boy. I'm only clumsy because I'm nervous trying to get everything right for everyone but me.'

What's it like to not be seen?

Pansy: I feel like I'm trapped under a rock or under the shell of a tortoise or a huge sea turtle and day by day I'm getting sucked further and further inside the turtle's dark belly. Sometimes I feel like I can't breathe properly, as if all the 'him', 'he' and 'Simons' build up around me like a thick shield that doesn't protect me but suffocates me. I feel lost and very alone in there.

But when people call out 'Pansy', I smile and instantly feel the fresh air on my face. It makes me want to climb to the top of a tall tree and reach the clouds, although I'm terrified of climbing!

I feel alive with the name Pansy. I feel confident and not nervous. As Simon I don't do very much because I'm too scared, but as Pansy I do whatever I want. I sing – a chorus of a song in assembly – I run and play, and I send artworks into competitions I see on television programmes like *Blue Peter* and *Vision On*. There is no stopping Pansy, there is no starting Simon.

Where are you happiest and why?

Pansy: I'm happiest when I can find quiet spaces outside in nature where I can close my eyes and dream about my life being different, about being Pansy all the time and a life in which I'd been born Pansy.

At night-time I sometimes dream that when I wake up in the morning things will have changed and that no one will think I'm a boy anymore. I wish that when my teacher asked me what I wanted to be when I grew up and I said, 'A mother like my mother' and that I wanted a belly full of babies, the class hadn't laughed and said, 'Don't be stupid. You're a boy and boys can't have babies even if you are a pansy.'

When I go to quiet places – the step by the rockery in the garden, or a branch in a tree – I close my eyes and imagine being the me inside that I feel is the one that nobody in the world ever sees. I wonder what my life might be like if I got the chance to be me properly. I know the other children laugh at me. I know my teacher is being nice, but being Pansy at school has made me realise that they are who I am inside.

What do you imagine you might be when you grow up?

Pansy: A mother. I've already said. Weren't you listening?

I was, sorry.

Pansy: And I want to write stories about the places I visit in my mind. Places that are fun, interesting and safe. Places where there is no space between me and the world.

If you could change one thing about your life now that might make it easier for you, what would it be?

Pansy: I would ask my teacher to call me by my real name (Pansy, obviously) off the carpet and also not to use my name to tell me off with.

Can you explain that a bit more?

Pansy: Sometimes she says that if I talk during a story (I never do) or play around with someone else from the class (I never do), then she will take away my name as it is a privilege and not a right. I don't think she means it horribly, I just think that she thinks calling me Pansy is a game, a bit of fun. She doesn't realise that it makes me come alive and that I cling on to her stories and never want them to end because I get to be me. When she threatens to take away my name, it makes everything feel like it could be blown away like a feather.

What would you say to those people who want to take away your identity and lock you away behind a shell?

Pansy: Please don't. I can't be happy if I'm not being me. Simple.

* *

Afterword

Gender Explorers is a brilliant book, especially if you want to get to know the wonderful thoughts of trans, nonbinary and gender diverse young people that bit better. As Juno says in the book, we're 'silenced by the way that [trans young people] are navigating the complexities of life itself and handling the complex pressures of gender expectations and stereotypes'. If this book shows anything, it's that they're not only navigating those complexities, but they seem to be doing it with gusto and happiness.

While of course it's right to stand up for trans children and young people, are these young people even calling themselves 'transgender', or even considering how much weight that word can hold in a world populated with grumps and naysayers? Juno makes an excellent case that what it is to be trans is all too often shaped by adult discussions and ideas, made out to be something more intense and 'other' than it really is. These are just children being children. We have no idea how any of them will turn out, how they'll identify or present in the future, but that's the entire point. These 'gender explorers' are just being themselves and trying to reach happiness in a world that often tries to minimise them.

At Gendered Intelligence, all we do is meet trans children where they are and give them space to be themselves and with others who may be like them, so they know they're not alone in whatever it is they're going through.

Some of them may choose to transition in any way that's right for them and we'll hold them in a supportive place if they do, but it's not our *raison d'être*. They may not even know it, but these young people are smashing the patriarchy every single day. As one young person says, 'just be yourself; and if anyone asks you why you aren't being stereotypical, just say that being trans is about overcoming stereotypes. Just live your best life.'

Seeing trans-affirmative spaces – such as Gendered Intelligence – provide to young people figuring out what their future dreams are is something to behold. When they're able to fully be themselves, you can see such a wild difference. Loved and supported trans young people turn into loved and supported trans adults in front of our eyes.

Thank you to Juno for bringing their words and experiences to a wider audience, and for giving voice to a group of people it's all too easy to sidestep. As one young person wonderfully summed up, when gender diverse people are given time and space to just be themselves, 'it's like you can let out a breath you've been holding in for ages.' So, here's to many more years of this freedom, and of books like *Gender Explorers* bringing the beauty and strength of trans power to everyone. From Gendered Intelligence, we can definitely recommend this book as a big stepping-stone on anyone's journey to learn about trans youth. Thank you.

Cara English and Jay Stewart, Gendered Intelligence

Gendered Intelligence is a charity that works with the trans community and those who impact on trans lives; we particularly specialise in supporting young trans people from the ages of 8–30.

We deliver trans youth programmes, support for parents and carers, professional development and trans awareness training for all sectors and educational workshops for schools, colleges, universities and other educational settings.

Our mission is to increase understandings of gender diversity.

Our vision is of a world where people are no longer constrained by narrow perceptions and expectations of gender, and where diverse gender expressions are visible and valued.

Resource Guide

Support and Advice

The following is an updated list of organisations, support groups and voluntary organisations across the country and including Scotland, Wales and Northern Ireland.

Making contact with a group can be daunting but getting support is vital and nourishing for you and those around you as you undertake your journey. It may be that you already have a great network for emotional support but that you need some more social space with other trans people your own age. Many of the following have social spaces and youth groups, some run weekend retreats and many offer support groups for parents and carers and wider family members.

Don't ever feel that you cannot contact more than one group, this is about YOU and finding a space that is comfortable and works for YOU and YOUR personality. Your feeling comfortable and confident in a space is the most important factor in finding and identifying the right kind of support. It may be that a two-hour youth group works for you right now whereas a weekend retreat might feel a little overwhelming but may not further down the road.

Go at your own pace, discover at your own pace and know, deep down, that this journey is yours to shape and create.

AKT (formally the Albert Kennedy Trust)
https://www.akt.org.uk
A nationwide LGBTQ+ homelessness charity providing advocacy and training in addition to housing.

Allsorts
https://www.allsortsyouth.org.uk
A Brighton-based organisation supporting and empowering young people who are LGBTQ+.

Distinction
https://www.distinctionsupport.org
A group to help people navigate their partner's transition with them.

Gender Agenda
www.genderagenda.net
A Norfolk-based training and education organisation focussing on trans, gender diverse and intersex people.

Gender Essence
www.genderessence.org.uk
Northern Ireland counselling organisation specialising in working with gender variant people.

Gendered Intelligence
http://genderedintelligence.co.uk
A nationwide, trans-led charity, delivering trans youth work, school mentoring, art projects, training and policy work.

GeneraTe
https://www.generateyork.org
Yorkshire-based support and social group for trans people and their families.

GIRES
https://www.gires.org.uk
Volunteer-run charity delivering training and information to give voice to trans and gender diverse people.

Intercom Trust/YAY Cornwall
https://www.intercomtrust.org.uk and
www.lgbtqyouthcornwall.co.uk
Youth groups for LGBTQ+ young people in Cornwall.

LGBT Foundation in Manchester
https://lgbt.foundation
A Manchester-based charity who support the needs of the diverse range of people who identify as lesbian, gay, bisexual and trans.

LGBT Health and Wellbeing
https://www.lgbthealth.org.uk
Offers support and social events for LGBT people, with specific trans and nonbinary events, to improve the wellbeing of the community across Scotland.

LGBT Youth Scotland

https://www.lgbtyouth.org.uk
Scotland's national charity for LGBTQI young people, offering support groups, advocacy and training.

Mermaids

https://www.mermaidsuk.org.uk
Mermaids hosts a support group for parents/carers of young gender variant people, as well as services and campaigning for those children themselves.

Mindline Trans+

https://bristolmind.org.uk/help-and-counselling/mindline-transplus
UK-wide phone service offering mental health and emotional support to gender diverse people who need it.

MindOut

www.mindout.org.uk
Brighton-based mental health organisation serving the LGBTQ+ community.

National Trans Youth Network

https://www.ntyn.org.uk
Representing all the trans youth groups across the UK.

Not Alone Plymouth

www.notaloneplymouth.co.uk
A support group for trans, including nonbinary, people in Plymouth.

Outline
https://outlinesurrey.org.uk
Surrey-based support organisation for people of any
sexuality or gender identity.

Sparkle
https://www.sparkle.org.uk
A nationwide group and events-based trans organisation.

TAGS
https://bit.ly/38BJn6v
Swimming, yoga and self-defence sessions for trans and
nonbinary people.

The Focus Trust
https://www.thefocustrust.com
Supporting trans and intersex people in NI, the Focus Trust
runs support groups and a buddying service.

Trans Can Sport
https://www.transcansport.co.uk
A Brighton-based not-for-profit providing free and low-
cost fitness sessions.

TransForum Manchester
www.transforum-manchester.co.uk
Peer support group for gender diverse people in the
Manchester area.

Transgender NI
https://transgenderni.org.uk
Support and advocacy group based in Belfast, running trans
support groups and the UK's only trans community centre.

Trans* Jersey
https://transjersey.org
A support group and advocacy organisation for gender
diverse people on Jersey.

TransLondon
www.translondon.org.uk
London-based support group for all trans and gender
diverse people with an active Facebook presence.

Trans Mission
https://www.uktransmission.org/wp
Organisation offering support groups (including a trans-
masculine and wellbeing group) and foodbank scheme in
Bradford, Leeds and Doncaster.

TransPals
http://transpals.org.uk
A Croydon social support group for trans people, working
across all of London.

Transpire
http://transpiresouthend.org
Transpire is a Southend-based organisation that hosts
support and discussion groups for trans people, their
friends and family.

Unique

www.uniquetg.org.uk

A trans-led support and befriending organisation working in North Wales and West Cheshire. Offering monthly meetings and community outreach.

Wise Thoughts

https://wisethoughts.org

Creating art initiatives and delivering services to address social justice issues for the LGBTQI+ and BAME communities.

Yorkshire MESMAC

https://www.mesmac.co.uk

A health, wellbeing and HIV-focussed organisation which also runs LGBTQI+ youth groups, mental health support and work with older LGBTQI+ people.